The Wind Band ▮▮▮▮
of Holst,
Vaughan Williams,
and Grainger

WILLIS M. RAPP

Published by
MEREDITH MUSIC PUBLICATIONS
a division of G.W. Music, Inc.
4899 Lerch Creek Ct., Galesville, MD 20765
http://www.meredithmusic.com

MEREDITH MUSIC PUBLICATIONS and its stylized double M logo are trademarks of
MEREDITH MUSIC PUBLICATIONS, a division of G.W. Music, Inc.

Text design and composition by Shawn Girsberger
Additional editing by James F. Keene

Library of Congress Control Number: 2004118093

Copyright © 2005 MEREDITH MUSIC PUBLICATIONS
International Copyright Secured • All Rights Reserved
First Edition
February 2005

International Standard Book Number: 1-57463-038-5
Printed and bound in U.S.A

This book is dedicated to
James R. Wells
Richard G. Wells
in recognition of their teaching, guidance,
and support of music education

CONTENTS

INTRODUCTION

In his Recorder Tutor **The Fontegara** *(1535 Venice)*, Sylvestro Ganassi states: *"Be it known that all musical instruments in comparison to the human voice are inferior to it. For this reason, we should endeavor to learn from it and imitate it."* Since that time, it has often been said that the human voice is the most perfect of all the instruments. Pedagogically, there has been a renewed emphasis on using the voice in the teaching of instrumental music. Pitch discrimination, ear training and interpretive phrasing are all achieved more easily with the voice, and subsequently can be transferred to instruments.

Throughout history, vocal/choral pieces have been used as source material for wind band works. This book has grown out of research that originally investigated the relationship of vocal/choral music to selected wind band masterworks of Gustav Holst, Ralph Vaughan Williams, and Percy Aldridge Grainger. While that focus remains an important part of this publication, the research has been expanded to include additional significant works for wind band composed by Holst, Vaughan Williams and Grainger.

The selection of repertoire for this book has been based on several points of view. On 11 July 1798, President John Adams signed an Act of Congress that established the United States Marine Band of 32 fifes and drums. Two centuries later on 11 July 1998, "The President's Own" marked the occasion with a concert at the John F. Kennedy Center for the Performing Arts. An interesting note is that this historic concert included performances of the Vaughan Williams *English Folk Song Suite* and Percy Grainger's *Marching Song of Democracy*, which represents two composers researched in this publication.

The 1967 Ph.D. Dissertation (The University of Iowa) by Eric Acton Ostling, Jr., *An Evaluation of Compositions for Wind Band According to Specific Criteria of Serious Artistic Merit*, and the more recent 1993 DMA Dissertation (Northwestern University) by Jay Warren Gilbert, *An Evaluation of Compositions for Wind Band According to Specific Criteria of Serious Artistic Merit; A Replication and Update*, contain seven of the selected wind band masterworks. The formula for ranking these works developed by Ostling and replicated by Gilbert reveals percentages of 87% for Vaughan Williams, 91% for Holst, and 100% for Grainger. The percentages clearly demonstrate an extremely high degree of receptivity among the twenty evaluators who participated in each study.

In 1997, authors Larry Blocher, Ray Cramer, Eugene Corporon, Tim Lautzenheiser, Edward S. Lisk, and Richard Miles (Editor and Complier) published *Teaching Music through Performance in Band*. The series is described as a resource that provides theoretical, analytical and practical information for band directors desiring to help students move beyond the printed page towards musical awareness and understanding. The first three volumes contain 300 of the best known and respected band compositions, and include eight of the wind band masterworks selected for this publication.

Finally, the experience of this author, who has served as a band director at the University level and guest conductor for nearly 30 years, immediately recognizes all of these masterworks as a must for any serious wind conductor's rotating repertoire list. Many of the works are also quite popular with guest conductors at honor band festivals throughout the nation. The common "thread" in several of these works is the composers' use of folk songs as well as folk dance tunes as source material. The exact relationship of each folk song to the wind band masterwork selected will be explored using a chronological approach.

Readers are encouraged to refer to the wind band full scores used for this study in order to make immediate comparisons between the original source material and its application to each wind band masterwork. Through this process, it is hoped that a deeper understanding of the music as well as additional insights into interpretation may be reached. **Chapter IV** contains the complete texts of all of the folk songs presented in this study.

For those who enjoy the works of Holst, Vaughan Williams, and Grainger there is an appreciation for the tireless work of these composers in their quest to use folk song sources in several of their compositions. While Holst, Vaughan Williams, and Grainger all spent some time collecting folk songs, it is also important to recognize some of the individuals who, either directly or indirectly, were of great assistance to this process. We refer to these individuals as the great English Folk Song collectors.

Lucy Etheldred Broadwood (1858-1929) A collector of English Folk Songs, Lucy was the niece of the Rev. John Broadwood (1798-1864), a pioneer folk song collector of Lyne in Sussex. Lucy collected folk songs in Surrey, Sussex, southern Ireland and the highlands of Scotland. She was a founder-member and subsequently secretary and editor of the *Journal of the Folk-Song Society*. These journals, published from 1898-1931, contain many songs collected and extensively annotated by Miss Broadwood, and show her wide knowledge of folklore, religious history and broadside ballads, as well as music in general.[1]

Maud Karpeles (1885-1976) At age twenty-four, while attending the Shakespeare festival at Stratford-on-Avon, she and her sister Helen encountered the Morris Dance being taught by Cecil Sharp. This was the beginning of an association that lasted until Sharp's death in 1924 and led to a lifetime of collecting and studying songs and dances, writing books and serving in national and international organizations. In 1911 Sharp founded the **English Folk Dance Society** and the Karpeles sisters became key figures in its organization. After Sharp's death, Karpeles served with Vaughan Williams as advisor to Douglas Kennedy, the newly appointed advisor of the **English Folk Dance Society**. Maud Karpeles wrote Cecil Sharp's biography in 1933 and a revised edition in 1967. In 1929 and 1930 she visited Newfoundland, thus realizing one of Sharp's aims; she collected 91 songs, of which she selected 30 for settings with piano accompaniments by Vaughan Williams, and others. In 1973, she published the definitive collection of Cecil Sharp's English Folksongs.[2]

Cecil James Sharp (1859-1924) An English folk music collector and editor, he was educated at Uppingham and Clare College, Cambridge. He began working in Australia, and in 1892 returned to England and became music master at Ludgrove Preparatory School; then in 1896 principal of the Hamstead Conservatory, a post he held until 1905. Two events turned his attention to folk music: on Boxing Day (traditionally, the day after Christmas, when the Lord of the Manor "boxed" the leftovers for the servants) 1899, he saw the Headington Morris side at Oxford dance *Laudnum Bunches* and four other traditional dances; and in the summer of 1903, while staying at Hambridge, Somerset, he heard a gardener sing "The Seeds of Love" as he mowed a lawn. He quickly realized the potential significance and value of the traditional arts, and thereafter devoted his life with missionary fervor to their preservation and propagation.[3]

As part of the introduction to the revised fourth edition of Cecil Sharp's book *English Folk Song: Some Conclusions*, Dr. Ralph Vaughan Williams offered in February 1954 several statements, many of which could be applied to the relevancy of this publication.

> It is not mere accident that the sudden emergence of vital invention among our English composers corresponds in time with this resuscitation of our own national melody. Of course there has been a reaction. The younger generation declare that folk songs had no influence on them. But much as they may dislike it, they can no more help being influenced by these melodies which have permeated the concert room, the school room, the stage and even the Church, than they can help speaking their own language... It is something which has persisted through the centuries, something which still appeals to us here and now and, if we allow it, will continue to develop through all the changes of history.[4]

Clearly, there is much to be learned from an in-depth study of the folk songs that inspired some of the great wind band masterworks of Gustav Holst, Ralph Vaughan Williams, and Percy Aldridge Grainger.

ENDNOTES

1. Stanley Sadie, ed., *The New Grove Dictionary of Music and Musicians*, vol. 3, *Lucy Etheldred Broadwood*, by Frank Howes (London: MacMillan Publishers Limited, 1980), 325.

2. Stanley Sadie, ed., *The New Grove Dictionary of Music and Musicians*, vol. 9, *Maud Karpeles*, by Frank Howes (London: MacMillan Publishers Limited, 1980), 813.

3 Stanley Sadie, ed., *The New Grove Dictionary of Music and Musicians,* vol. 17, *Cecil James Sharp,* by Frank Howes (London: MacMillan Publishers Limited, 1980), 231.

4 Ralph Vaughan Williams, foreword to *English Folk Song: Some Conclusions,* by Cecil J. Sharp (Belmont, CA: Wadsworth Publishing Company, Inc., 1965), viii, ix.

Gustav Holst

CHAPTER
ONE 🖋

GUSTAV HOLST (b. Cheltenham, 21 September 1874; d. London, 25 May 1934), received his musical education at the Royal College of Music beginning in 1893. During this time, he formed an abiding friendship with Ralph Vaughan Williams, which had a pronounced influence upon his career.[1] Even up to the time of his death, Holst and Vaughan Williams would regularly spend time together, and each would try out their compositions on one another. In reference to Holst's last work for Military Band, *Hammersmith Prelude and Scherzo, Op. 52*, there is a record of him trying out the work with Vaughan Williams on 12 December, 1930.[2]

First Suite in E-flat for Military Band, Opus 28 No. 1

Composed:	1909, Copyright 1921 by Boosey & Co., London. Full Score edition 1948 by Boosey & Co. (with additional parts for American Band Instrumentation)
Duration:	c. 10 minutes
First Performance:	1920, (Royal Military School of Music at Kneller Hall, Royal Albert Hall, London.)
Revised Edition:	by Colin Matthews 1984, published by Boosey & Co. Ltd.

Without doubt, the person who can provide the best understanding of where Holst was in his journey as a composer at the time of his *First Suite in E-flat for Military Band* would be his daughter, Imogen. Imogen Holst wrote a book on her father's music in 1948–50, at a time where very little of his music had even been recorded, except for *The Planets*, short works such as the *St. Paul's Suite* and ballet music from

The Perfect Fool. In the fifteen years that passed from her publication, there was a dramatic increase in both the popularity as well as the accessibility of Holst's music. In 1967, Oxford University Press wisely pressed Imogen for permission to produce a photographic reproduction of the out of print book. Imogen agreed, and also added some material. In 1968, the second edition of *The Music of Gustav Holst* was released.

Of his first composition for Military Band Imogen Holst writes, "the *First Suite in Eb* was an experiment in form, each movement being founded on a fragment of the opening Chaconne. He was in his second apprenticeship: having learned that symphonic development and leitmotif were equally hopeless for his sort of tune, he was trying to find a form that would satisfy his own needs, and the Chaconne proves how far he had traveled since the first years of folk-song influence."[3]

A great deal of credit also goes to Colin Matthews who, in 1984, completed a revised critical edition of the composition which also corrected numerous errors from the 1948 full score edition. Unfortunately, the 1948 score had been prepared through the process of a compilation of the existing parts with no reference to the original manuscript score (now in the British Library, London, Add. MS 47824). While Colin Matthews did not seek the assistance of Frederick Fennell, Fennell is acknowledged in the preface of the revised 1984 edition as having provided invaluable assistance during the preparation of this edition. As a result, wind conductors who wish to rehearse and perform Holst's *First Suite in Eb for Military Band* should use the score and parts from the revised full score edition of 1984, available from Boosey & Hawkes.

Colin Matthews has taken great care to elucidate the various uses of the term *ad lib* as used by Holst in this composition, which still allows for performances of the *First Suite in Eb* by an ensemble as few as 19 players (plus percussion) if desired.

Flute & Piccolo	Solo Cornet
Solo Clarinet	1st Cornet
1st Clarinet	2nd Cornet
2nd Clarinet	1st & 2nd Horns in F
3rd Clarinet	1st Trombone
Bass Clarinet	3rd Trombone
1st Bassoon	Euphonium
Alto Saxophone	Bass
Tenor Saxophone	

The title page of the original manuscript score (of 1909) was completed by Holst in cursive handwriting on staff paper containing 28 staves. The lower third of this title page bears the following instructions: *As each movement is founded on the same phrase, it is requested that the Suite shall be played right through without a break. It is suggested that in the absence of a string bass, the ad lib part for that instrument in the Intermezzo shall not be played on any brass instrument, but omitted, excepting where the notes are cued in other parts. Also in the absence of Timpani, the ad lib part for the latter is to be omitted entirely.* These instructions were reprinted at the bottom of the condensed conductor's score in the original 1921 edition, but are curiously absent in the full conductor's score of 1948. An examination of the 1948 edition lists both the full score as well as the condensed score as part of the complete symphonic set of parts. However, with an increasing interest by wind band conductors over the last half of the twentieth century to use full scores, we have witnessed a practice of many conductors who perform Holst's *First Suite in Eb for Military Band* using the customary pauses found in other multi-movement suites, thus ignoring Holst's original performance intent.

In his book, *The Composers Advocate, A Radical Orthodoxy for Musicians*, Erich Leinsdorf sets forth some provocative theories on how to understand and perform music. Believing that great composers knew how they wanted their music to sound, he invites young conductors—indeed, all serious music lovers—to join him in discovering those composers' intentions. While all of Leinsdorf's specific examples deal with orchestral and operatic repertoire, the following passage probably best speaks to what has happened over the years regarding performances of Holst's *First Suite in Eb for Military Band*, "the regular application of a conductor's own intellect to the problems of music, from a fresh and unbiased perspective, is crucially important. Music has too long suffered from inertia. In human affairs, as in physics, inertia can be overcome only by energy. A concentration of intellectual energy is desperately needed to counteract our uncritical reliance on accumulated beliefs and customs, many of which are based on fallacies."[4] Clearly, we should not separate the three movements of Holst's *First Suite in Eb for Military Band*, and this fact is confirmed by the last statement in the introductory material found in the 1984 revised edition by Colin Matthews which states the three movements should be played without a break.

The first movement, **Chaconne**, is comprised of a melody which fulfills the exact definition of the term chaconne, "an instrumental piece consisting of a series of variations above a ground bass not over 8 measures in length, in a 3–4 time and slow tempo."[5] However, there has always been some debate as to whether the first movement of Holst's *Suite in Eb for Military Band* is really a chaconne or actually a passacaglia. Since both forms are derived from early Spanish dances, there is a fair amount of similarity. William Barclay Squire wrote the following as part of his article describing the passacaglia in the Grove Dictionary of Music, "the only material difference between the two seems to be that in the chaconne the theme is kept invariably in the bass, while in the passacaglia it was used in any part, often so disguised and embroidered amid ever-varying contrapuntal devices as to hardly remain recognizable."[6] The theme is initially presented in the euphonium and tuba parts (doubled in string bass), then proceeds to be passed to other sections of the wind band for a total of 16 different eight-measure variations.

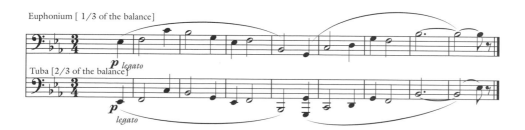

The following phrase chart has been designed for easy reference. Conductors are encouraged to mark study scores for use in rehearsal.

Phrase Chart – Chaconne

Measures	Music	Scoring
1–8	Chaconne Theme	Euphonium, Tuba (doubled in String Bass) in E♭ Major
9–16	Variation 1	Cornets, Trombones
17–24	Variation 2	Winds (doubled in String Bass)
25–32	Variation 3	Theme in Euphonium, Tuba (doubled in Baritone Sax) Counterstatement in Winds and Saxes
33–40	Variation 4	Theme in Low Brass, Low Reeds New Counterstatement in Winds, Saxes, Cornets, Horns
41–48	Variation 5	Theme in short note values in Brass, Low Saxes Sixteenth note Countermelody in Winds
49–56	Variation 6	Theme in Cornets, Horns *Pesante* Eighth Note line in Low Brass, Low Reeds
57–64	Variation 7	Theme in Solo Horn (doubled in 3rd Clarinet) Additional obligato parts in 1st & 2nd Clarinets
65–72	Variation 8	Theme in Solo Alto Sax Accompaniment in Solo Flute, Solo Oboe, E♭ Clarinet
73–80	Variation 9	Inversion of Theme in C Minor Scored in 1st & 2nd Horns (doubled in Alto Sax & 3rd Clar.) Accompaniment in upper Winds
81–88	Variation 10	Inversion of Theme in Cornets, Euphonium Bass line Accompaniment in Bassoons, Tuba

89–96	Variation 11	Presentation of original Theme in Trombones a minor third higher than originally written
97–104	Variation 12	Return of Original Theme in Euphonium in E♭ Major (doubled in 1st Cornet) Pedal B♭ sustained in Tuba, Low Reeds
105–113	Variation 13	Theme in Flute, Oboe, 1st Clarinet, 1st Cornet, 1st Horn with phrase extension (nine measures) Eighth note accompaniment in Clarinets and Saxes
114–121	Variation 14	Recapitulation of Theme scored as tutti
122–125	Variation 15	First Half of Theme in Cornets, Trombones
126–131	Variation 16	Coda based on Theme

Of particular interest in this first movement is Holst's ability to create 15 variations on the original theme which retain listener (and performer) interest through the techniques of orchestration, inversion, and transformation. It can be quite beneficial for students to have the opportunity to hear each variation played individually to compare and contrast the type of orchestration used by Holst in variations 2–8. In variation 9 the theme is inverted and set against the new harmony of C minor. Then, in variation 11 Holst takes the original theme, writes it a third higher and retains the C minor harmonization. The following musical example shows a comparison between the original theme as played by the Euphonium in measures 1–8 and how it compares to variation 11, played by the Trombones in measures 89–96.

This sets up a return of the original theme in E-flat Major, this time against a B-flat pedal in the tuba, bassoons, and bass clarinet. Since this pedal-tone continues through the next variation, it is important that care be taken not to build the crescendo too soon, and especially to wait until the very end (last three measures) to really build the upper instruments to a stunning climax to set off the beginning of variation 14. From here to the end of the movement there can be no turning back, and the players must make the commitment to play through the notes, use full breath support, but not overplay the end of the movement.

The second movement, *Intermezzo*, is comprised of two principal themes. Set at the tempo of *vivace*, this second movement serves a function of connecting the slow, stately first movement to the third movement which is set in the tempo of a march. But, much more than a providing a simple connection between longer movements (as the title intermezzo suggests), it stands as the central movement in the suite, providing a light staccato theme (measures 3–66) balanced by a contrasting legato theme (measures 67–98). Within the light staccato theme, there is a 16 measure section (measures 27–42) which serves as a transition to connect a restatement of the light staccato theme. A full return to the light staccato theme (measures 101–122) is then balanced by a return of the contrasting legato theme (measures 123–134) with fragments of the light staccato theme as well as material based on a transition theme from the opening section of the movement.

Phrase Chart–Intermezzo

Measures	Music	Scoring
1–2	Introduction	E♭ Clarinets divisi (2nd part cued in 1st B♭ Clarinet)
3–26	Theme 1	Oboes, Solo B♭ Clarinet, Solo 1st Cornet: C minor
27–42	Transition	Clarinets with tutti crescendo
43–66	Theme 1	Repeated in Oboes, Solo B♭ Clarinet, Solo 1st Cornet
67	Transition	Clarinet Solo
68–83	Theme 2	Solo B♭ Clarinet
84–98	Theme 2	Repeated in Solo 1st Cornet, Solo Euphonium
99–100	Transition	Clarinets/Horns to Trombones
101–122	Theme 1	Varied in Euphonium, Woodwinds added in next phrase

123	Transition	Timpani, String Bass, Bassoon
124–134	Theme 2	Returns in Euphonium, Bass Clarinet, Low Saxes along with Transition Theme in Clarinets
135–138	Transition	Flutes & E♭ Clarinet
139–142	Coda	3-Note Fragment of Theme 1 in Trombone, then Horn, then Cornet, then Piccolo

The contrasting legato theme is first heard as a clarinet solo in measures 67–75, then joined by the solo flute in measures 76–83. For the repeat of this theme, Holst turns to Solo Cornet (measures 84–98) which is now doubled in Solo Euphonium in the 1984 Colin Matthews edition. Although this doubling does not appear in the 1948 full score edition, the decision by Colin Matthews to include this doubling is supported by information found on page 20 of the manuscript score, which reveals that Holst originally wrote this melody for the B-flat Baritone Horn part, a completely separate part from the Euphonium. Since the 1948 full score was prepared from an existing set of parts, this part was completely omitted until measure 96–98, precisely when Holst shifted the melody from the B♭ Baritone to the Euphonium part to end the phrase.

Euphonium [measures 83-98]

mf *dolce*

As can be seen from the economy of compositional style exhibited in the first movement, Holst uses the same theme transposed down a minor third when it appears as a Euphonium solo near the end of the movement in measures 123–138.

The articulation is nearly identical to the previous passage, only this time we find a doubling in the Bass Clarinet part.

The final twenty measures of this movement should be of particular interest to wind conductors as well as student performers as Holst uses the first two measures of the light staccato theme (measures 128–129 and 132–133) as well as a one-measure fragment (measure 134) contrapuntally against the contrasting legato theme. He also uses the first two measures of the transition theme transposed a minor third lower (measures 126–127 and 130–131) before developing it as the final statement to end the movement (measures 135–142). This section alone can provide a fascinating study of pointillism as a compositional device.

The third movement, *March*, is constructed in the form of a march, complete with a trio and a "dogfight" section. After the four measure introduction, the first and second strains of the march are scored for brass and percussion only, with the woodwinds not entering until the trio section (measure 40). Conductors should note that the 1984 Colin Matthews edition contains a Euphonium part that is new to this edition, a Solo (ad lib.) line which is based on the B-flat Baritone part from the original manuscript score. Once again, since the 1948 full score was prepared from an existing set of parts, this line was completely omitted from measures 4–12. This is just another example of why it is important to invest in the 1984 edition full score and parts even if the 1948 edition is already in your library. And, for those students who are interested in learning more about the preparation of critical editions in music, a comparison of the full scores from the 1948 and 1984 editions is invaluable.

Phrase Chart – March

Measures	Music	Scoring
1–4	Introduction	Trills in Upper Woodwinds, Cornets to Low Brass
5–36	First Strain	Brass and Percussion: E-flat Major

37–40	Trio Begins	Solo Cymbal Crash, Sustained Brass, Moving Bass Line
41–70	Trio Melody	Winds (no flute or oboe), doubled in Horns: A-flat Major
71–88	Trio Melody	Repeated, with oboes and E♭ Clarinet added
89–96	False Recap	First Strain returns in Woodwinds
97–122	"Dogfight" Section	Builds with Progression of Minor Chromatic Chords
123–168	Recapitulation	First Strain Theme in Upper Woodwinds: E-flat Major Trio Theme in Low Brass
169–179	Coda	Cornets with Low Brass Accompaniment Trills in upper Woodwinds, Ends with a Flourish

Of particular interest in this movement is Holst's choice of melodic material for use in the Trio section (beginning in measure 40), which is based on the Chaconne Theme from the first movement. This economical approach to the use of melodic material can also be seen as Holst using material from the middle section of the first strain (measures 13–16) to develop a "dogfight" section from measures 97–122. However, the original material (in E-flat Major) begins in C minor, and cleverly modulates chromatically upward by half step to resolve back to E-flat Major in measure 109. As the intensity of the music increases from measures 109–122, one will hear in several of the recordings by Frederick Fennell an additional motive added in the timpani part in measure 118, which doubles the pitches of F, Eb, and G already found in the low brass parts. Since the solo bass drum has just been heard in measure 116–117, this added timpani part has a way of connecting to the entrance of the snare drum in measure 119 as well as adding more excitement to the low brass answer in measure 118.

Holst brings everything together in masterful fashion in the recapitulation section beginning in measure 123. Here we find the first strain theme from the opening of the movement combined with the trio theme as the movement returns to E-flat major. When the middle section of the first strain theme appears as part of the recapitulation (beginning in measure 131), we notice that Holst adjusts the steady quarter note rhythm of the original to include an eight note triplet embellishment (see measures 133–134). Once again, economy is at work with just enough change to keep the work fresh and forward moving. The Coda is constructed using the same rhythm of the motive from the middle section of the first strain theme.

ENDNOTES

1. Stanley Sadie, ed., *The New Grove Dictionary of Music and Musicians,* vol. 8, *Gustav Holst,* by Imogen Holst (London: MacMillan Publishers Limited, 1980), 659.

2. Jon C. Mitchell, "Gustav Holst: The Hammersmith Sketches," *CBDNA Journal* (1986): 13.

3. Imogen Holst, 2nd Rev. ed. *The Music of Gustav Holst* (London: Oxford University Press, 1968), 34.

4. Erich Leinsdorf, *The Composer's Advocate, A Radical Orthodoxy for Musicians* (New Haven: Yale University Press, 1981), 23.

5. Theodore Baker, ed., *Pronouncing Pocket-Manual of Musical Terms* (New York: G. Schirmer, 1947), 44.

6. Eric Blom, ed., *Grove's Dictionary of Music and Musicians,* vol. 6, *Passacaglia,* by William Barclay Squire (London: MacMillan & Co., Ltd., 1954), 575.

Second Suite in F for Military Band, Opus 28 No. 2

Composed: 1911, Copyright 1922 by Boosey & Co., London.
Duration: c. 10 ½ minutes
First Performance: 30 June 1922 Royal Military School of Music at Kneller Hall,
                       Royal Albert Hall, London.
Revised Edition: by Colin Matthews 1984, published by Boosey & Co. Ltd.

Of his *Second Suite in F for Military Band* Gustav Holst writes, "this Suite is founded on old English Country tunes."[1] The suite has the unique distinction of having been created in 1911 as a work for wind band, with vocal arrangements of "Swansea Town," "I'll Love My Love," and "Song of the Blacksmith" following in 1917. These were published in a collection entitled *Six Choral Folk Songs, Op. 36*. Although Holst did the settings of these folk songs for chorus after he wrote the *Second Suite for Band*, the choral settings are most revealing in that the texts provide clues to interpreting the wind band music.[2]

The first movement, *March*, is comprised of a folk dance melody, "Morris Dance," as well as two folk songs, "Swansea Town," and "Claudy Banks." Credit for "Morris Dance" goes to Cecil J. Sharp and Herbert C. MacIlwaine for a folk tune titled *Glorishears*—Bampton Tradition, published by Novello & Co., Ltd. in 1910.

In examining a copy of Holst's original manuscript to the *Second Suite in F* (now in the British Library, London, Add. MS 47825), pages are included that show the first movement originally beginning with the folk tune "Young Reilly" in F Minor. A total of 38 measures of full score including a title page are included in this manuscript, then crossed out. Holst obviously changed his mind and revised the movement to begin with 46 measures of "Morris Dance" which are written on eight pages of score inserted as the beginning of the piece. This entire process must have been done with some haste as this new introduction makes use of *colla bars,* a practice often used by arrangers who are quickly completing sketches for orchestrators or copyists. Holst employed the use of capital letters from A through P to designate those measures which were to be repeated when engraved parts were prepared for the performers.[3]

After a short, one-measure motif introduced in euphonium and tuba, then repeated by upper woodwinds, the "Morris Dance" tune is presented in measures 3–18. With a few minor exceptions in rhythm and the obvious adjustment of key from D Major to F Major, the opening measures of the Morris Dance used by Holst are almost an exact replica of the Sharp and MacIlwaine original. After an interlude (measures 19–26), Holst repeats the "Morris Dance" tune with a phrase extension (measures 27–46), leading directly into "Swansea Town"(measures 47–110).

"Swansea Town," a Hampshire Folk Song came from a collection by Dr. G. B. Gardiner. Holst chose to set this poignant melody as a euphonium solo, and these two 16-measure phrases are still considered to be one of the finest moments for the euphonium in all of the wind band literature. In comparing Holst's approach to scoring in his collection of *Six Choral Folk Songs, Op. 36*, published by J. Curwen & Sons, Ltd. in 1917, we note "Swansea Town" arranged for Mixed Voices was also originally in D Major. The biggest change in this folk song (visually) is the departure from the use of 4/4 meter to Alla breve. This is strictly a notational issue in order to maintain continuity with the "Morris Dance" section. With the exception of two minor rhythmic alterations (compare measures 3 & 15 in original to measures 49 & 74 in the Suite), Holst retains the exact rhythmic character of the original.

A version of "Swansea Town" for Male Chorus arranged by Holst and recorded by the Baccholian Singers of London (*Bushes and Briars,* EMI Classics, CDMB 65123) certainly bears a striking resemblance in character to the euphonium solo scored from measures 46–78 in the *Second Suite*. In his sixth article on basic band repertory (*The Instrumentalist*, November 1977), Frederick Fennell selected Gustav Holst's *Second Suite in F for Military Band* as yet another representative piece of British

Military band music for a conductor's analysis. In this detailed article, Fennell provides the reader with a series of his interpretive markings for this 32 bar solo which *follow exactly* the interpretation used in this recording. This directly supports the position that knowledge of the words of the folk song as well as an understanding of the original use of the music shapes one's attitudes toward an acceptable musical interpretation for wind instruments.

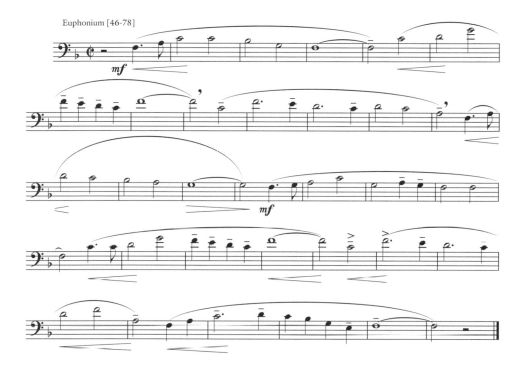

Euphonium [46-78]

The tune "Claudy Banks," as sung by Frederick White of Southampton, comprises the melodic material for the end of the first movement of the ***March***. Once again, we see a close relationship in the use of melodic material from the original 1909 Folk Song as noted by J. F. Guyer to Holst's treatment in the *Second Suite*. The shift in meter to 6/8, the key adjustment of E Aeolian to B♭ Dorian, and the strict adherence to the original rhythm characterize Holst's use of this folk song. A printed fermata in measure 10 of the original might suggest a point of stretching the phrase in performing the Suite (at measure 121).

Holst returns to the "Morris Dance" tune followed by "Swansea Town" to end the movement.

The second movement is curiously titled *Song Without Words*, yet bears the subtitle "I'll Love My Love." Holst used this Cornish Folk Song collected in Hampshire by G. B. Gardiner. While it is not clear from the original wind band manuscript whether Holst intended the solo at the beginning of the movement to be played by oboe or clarinet or both, a revised 1984 edition of the score by Colin Matthews (based on the autograph manuscript) presents what appear to be Holst's first thoughts: a clarinet solo, with the oboe not joining the melody until bar eleven.[4]

In comparing the melody of the Second Suite with Holst's arrangement for Mixed Voices, published in 1917 by J. Curwen & Sons, Inc., we see no apparent differences in the treatment of this tender melody. Both are set in F Dorian and the 16 measures exhibit an exact rhythmic match. A fermata is found in measure 14 of the choral score. While this interpretation is often imitated in the wind band performance, the score is marked only ad lib. at measure 16. For reference, the primary source for this folk song is taken from Vol. II of the *Journal of the Folk-Song Society*, 1905–1906, and is noted in D Dorian.

A - broad as I was walk - ing, one eve - ning in the spring. I heard a maid in Bed - lam so sweet-ly for to sing; Her chains she rat - tled with her hands, and thus re - plied she: I love my love be - cause I know my love loves me!

Listening to the Baccholian Singer's recording of the version set by Holst for Male Chorus reveals a tempo of ♩ = 118; quite a bit faster than one might take for wind band performance (♩ = 60). Considering Holst's use of eighth-note arpeggio figures (beginning in measure 18) for the second verse of the wind band score, this slower tempo is certainly most appropriate. Additionally, this folk song is intended for use as the second, or slow movement of this four movement Suite. This recording also reveals a shift in key to G minor for the Male Chorus.

Perhaps the most unique piece of Choral music is found in the third movement; **Song of the Blacksmith**, another Hampshire Folk Song collected by G. B. Gardiner and arranged in 1917 for Mixed Voices (G. Schirmer No. 10816) as well as Male Chorus (G. Schirmer No. 11828) by Holst. As we read the words, and even sing the tune, we are able at once to form a clear interpretative impression of Holst's concept for the third movement of this Suite which, regrettably, is often performed too fast (even though the tempo is marked Moderato e maestoso in both versions). It is suggested here that wind band conductors copy the words to the *Song of the Blacksmith* directly into their score (there is enough room if one writes some words above and others below either the Alto Sax or Horn parts in measures 6–14) and sing the song to the performers just prior to rehearsing this movement.

Once the wind performers hear the opening line of "kang, kang, kang ki ki kang, kang kang, ki ki kang kang," vocalized, they are better able to form an image of this imposing, brawny man, covered with sweat, wearing a large leather apron to shield his huge torso from the sparks of his persistent hammering.[5] This is typical of the kind of imagery that certainly inspires interpretative performances.

Kang kang kang ki ki kang
kang kang ki ki kang kang

For the blacksmith courted me,
nine months and better;
And first he won my heart,

till he wrote to me a letter.
With his hammer in his hand,
for he strikes so mighty and clever,
He makes the sparks to fly
all round his middle.

Holst adjusts the key signature from F Major in the 1911 Wind Score to G Major for use in the 1917 Mixed Voices arrangement, this being consistent with what we might expect when a piece originally written for band instruments is adapted for voices. Actually, the chord progression of the two-measure ostinato centers around G Dorian, while the melody is performed in D Aeolian, G Aeolian, and D Aeolian.[6] Structurally, the two versions match in length (33 measures each), rhythmic organization (alternating measures of 4/4 and 3/4 in the opening), and phrase structure. How interesting it is to observe that the power and intensity of this particular Hampshire Folk Song moved Holst to keep every detail intact from the wind band to the choral version.

In listening to the version for Male Chorus performed by the Baccholian Singers of London, a tempo of ♩ = 108 is heard. This tempo allows for clear diction, considering the text of this folk song. A slightly slower tempo of ♩ = 96–100, seems to be consistent with recorded wind band performances by Frederick Fennell and others, perhaps favoring the imagery of the brawny blacksmith.

The fourth movement, **Fantasia on the Dargason**, is almost identical with the Finale of **St. Paul's Suite** for String Orchestra, published by Goodwin & Tabb.[7] The "Dargason" tune can be traced to *The Dancing Master* (1650–51), and is comprised of an eight-measure tune which ends on the fifth of the key, producing a melody that seems to be never ending. The tune is one of those which only ends when the singer is exhausted![8]

Holst sets this movement as an eight-measure theme with a subsequent set of five variations before the traditional English tune "Greensleeves" (variants include 'Green Sleaves' and 'Green Sleeves') is introduced into the musical score. The earliest mention of the ballad of *Green Sleeves* is in September, 1580, when Richard Jones had licensed to him, "A new Northern Dittye of the *Lady Green Sleeves*." Within twelve days of the first entry it was converted to a pious use, and we have, *"Green Sleeves mortalised to the Scripture, declaring the manifold benefits and blessings of God bestowed on sinful man."*[9]

Λ - las my love - you do me wrong, To cast me off - dis - court-eous-ly And

I have loved - you for so long, De - light - ing in - your com - pan-y.

Green - sleeves-was all my joy   Green   sleeves   was   my de-light   Green - sleeves was my

heart   of   gold,   And   who   but   my   lad - y   Green - sleeves

In all, there are 25 complete statements of the eight-measure "Dargason" tune.[10] Holst demonstrates his compositional expertise as he cleverly sets the "Greensleeves" theme against the "Dargason" melody. By transposing the original "Greensleeves" tune from E Dorian to G Dorian and introducing this tune beginning in the third measure of the "Dargason" tune (measure 59 in the wind score) Holst is able to bring both tunes together in harmonic agreement. By changing the meter in Solo/1st B-flat Clarinet and Euphonium from 6/8 to 3/4 and smoothing out the original rhythm of "Greensleeves," Holst creates a version that makes better sense in the contrapuntal setting as seen in measures 59–96.

One final question to be considered is whether or not Holst intended to emulate the mood of all of the texts selected for this wind band masterpiece. In the case of "Swansea Town" and "Song of the Blacksmith," one can immediately see a direct correlation between the text and the stylistic direction that the music should take. Looking at "Claudy Banks" and "Greensleeves", however, might lead us to different conclusions. To understand the story behind the folk song "Claudy Banks," one must read all eight stanzas of the text.

> As I roved out one evening all in the month of May,
> Down by the Banks of Claudy I carelessly did stray,
> There I beheld a young maid in sorrow did complain,
> Lamenting of her true Love who had crossed the raging main.
>
> *Chorus.* Io, Io, he is my darling boy,
> He is the darling of my heart upon the walls of Troy.
>
> I steppéd up unto her and gave her a great suprise.
> I won she did not know me, for I was in disguise.
> I said, "My pretty fair maid, my joy and heart's delight,
> How far do you mean to wander this dark and dreary night?"
>   Io, Io, etc.
>
> It's on the Banks of Claudy I wish you would me show
> Take on a fair young maid who has nowhere to go,

For I am in search of a young man, young Johnny is his name,
And on the Banks of Claudy I hear he does remain."
    Io, Io, etc.

"This is the Banks of Claudy, on them you now do stand,
Do not believe young Johnny, for he's a false young man.
Do not believe young Johnny, he will not meet you here,
Through the green woods you may tarry, no danger you may fear."
    Io, Io, etc.

"Oh if my Johnny were here to-night, he would keep me from all harm,
But he's on the field of battle and in his uniform.
He's on the field of battle, all danger he does defy,
Like the royal king of honour upon the walls of Troy.
    Io, Io, etc.

It's six long months, and better, since my Johnny left the shore
To cross the raging ocean where thundering billows roar,
To cross the raging ocean for honour and for fame."
"I heard the ship was wrecked upon the coasts of Spain."
    Io, Io, etc.

As soon as she heard this, she fell in deep despair,
A-wringing of her lily-white hands and a-tearing of her hair,
Saying, "If my Johnny's drownded, no other man I'll take,
Through lonesome woods and valleys will I wander for his sake."
    Io, Io, etc.

As soon as he had heard this, no longer could he stand;
He flew into her arms, saying, "Betsy, I'm the man."
Saying, "Betsy, I'm the young man who caused your grief and pain,
And since we've met on Claudy's fair Banks, we never will part again."
    Io, Io, etc.

While most of this text suggests a sorrowful situation, Holst uses the tune in a different manner. In the case of "Claudy Banks," he is following "Swansea Town," the text of which portrays a sense of optimism in parting situation. As the *da capo* form returns to the high spirited "Morris Dance," one can assume that Holst was primarily interested in linking three folk songs together on the merit of their melodic, harmonic and rhythmic interest; therefore, being less concerned about the implications of the textual differences between the last two tunes. The same is true for the five stanzas of "Greensleeves."

Alas my love you do me wrong,
To cast me off discourteously;
And I have loved you for so long,
Delighting in your company.

Chorus. Greensleeves was all my joy,
Greensleeves was my delight,
Greensleeves was my heart of gold,
And who but my lady Greensleeves.

I long have waited at your hand
To do your bidding as your slave,
And waged, have I, both life and land

Your love and affection for to have.
  Greensleeves…

If you intend thus to distain
It does the more enrapture me,
And even so, I will remain
Your lover in captivity.
  Greensleeves…

Alas, my love, that yours should be
A heart of faithless vanity,
So here I mediate alone
Upon your insincerity.
  Greensleeves…

Ah, Greensleeves, now farewell, adieu,
To God I pray to prosper thee,
For I remain thy lover true,
Come once again and be with me.

The use of "Greensleeves" in the fourth movement seems to point to a situation where Holst was seeking a good contrapuntal match for the "Dargason" theme, and less concerned that we might use the text to influence our interpretation in this particular context.

One of the greatest benefits of studying the original source material is in the area of discovering the texts of these folk songs. A simple reading of the text helps to immediately convey the meaning of the music to the performers. Barry Green, in *The Inner Game of Music,* talks about the power of will in finding the meaning of the music as a performance goal. "Some musical pieces… are 'program' pieces, written to express a specific atmosphere or story in sound. Most instrumental music, however, is not. To give your performance a new sense of conviction and color, you can create your own 'program' for a piece of music."[11] The possibility of studying the authentic style of Holst's *Second Suite in F for Military Band* begins with knowing, or at least hearing the text of each folk song.

The *Second Suite in F for Military Band* is one of five little masterpieces (the total contributions of Holst and Vaughan Williams) which are unquestionably considered basic to the repertory of wind bands.[12]

ENDNOTES

1. Imogen Holst, 2nd Rev. ed. *The Music of Gustav Holst* (London: Oxford University Press, 1968), 34.

2. Robert J. Garofalo, *Guides to Band Masterworks* (Ft. Lauderdale, FL: Meredith Music Publications, 1992), 61–63.

3. Gustav Holst, "Second Suite for Military band in F, op.28 no. 2," facsimile of the manuscript score, 1911, submitted by the composer to Boosey & Co., London.

4. Gustav Holst, *Second Suite in F*, Revised Edition by Colin Matthews (London: Boosey & Hawkes, 1984), ii.

5. Robert J. Garofalo, *Guides to Band Masterworks* (Ft. Lauderdale, FL: Meredith Music Publications, 1992), 72.

6. Richard Miles, ed., *Teaching Music Through Performance in Band* (Chicago: GIA Publications, Inc., 1997), 289.

7. Gustav Holst, *Second Suite for Military Band in F Major*, Condensed Score (London: Boosey & Co., 1922), 2.

8. William Chappell, *Popular Music in the Olden Time* (New York: Dover Publications, 1965), 64–65.

9. William Chappell, *Popular Music in the Olden Time* (New York: Dover Publications, 1965), 227–228.

10. Robert J. Garofalo, *Guides to Band Masterworks* (Ft. Lauderdale, FL: Meredith Music Publications, 1992), 65.

11. Barry Green, *The Inner Game of Music* (New York: Doubleday, 1986), 61–62.

12. Frederick Fennell, "Gustav Holst's Second Suite in F for Military Band," *The Instrumentalist* (1977): 42.

Hammersmith Prelude and Scherzo, Opus 52

Composed:	1930, Transcribed for Orchestra 1931. Copyright (for Band) 1956 by Hawkes & Son, Ltd., London. Copyright renewed 1984
Duration:	c. 13 1/2 minutes
First Orchestral Performance:	25 November 1931 by the B.B.C. Symphony Orchestra at Queens Hall, London, Adrian Boult conducting.
First Band Performance:	17 April 1932 by the United States Marine Band, Capt. Taylor Branson conducting at the American Bandmasters Association Convention in Washington, D.C.
Second Band Performance:	14 April 1954 by the Kiltie Band of the Carnegie Institute of Technology (now Carnegie Mellon University), Robert Cantrick conducting.
Corrected Edition:	1986 by Boosey & Hawkes.

The year 1930 was considered to be one of Holst's best years for composing. He brought all of his energy to the works he had been commissioned to compose, the *Choral Fantasia*, written for the Three Choirs Festival, and *Hammersmith*, a Prelude and Scherzo commissioned by the BBC Military Band. Of important note is that the BBC Military Band was a professional band, not the student military bands for which Holst had composed his earlier suites. It is little wonder that we hear so few performances of Holst's *Hammersmith*, as the work demands the maturity level generally found in wind bands at the college and university level.

Imogen Holst wrote of her father's approach to the work, "the mood out of which the music had grown was a mood that had haunted him for nearly forty years: during his solitary walks in Hammersmith he had always been aware of the aloofness of the quiet river, unhurried and unconcerned, while just round the corner there was all the noise and hustle and exuberant vulgarity of the cockney crowd, pushing and shoving and sweating and swearing and shrieking and guffawing its good-humored way."[1]

Hammersmith was named after the western metropolitan borough of London, where for the last twenty-nine years of his life, Holst had made his working headquarters at the St. Paul's Girls' School. As the music director of the St. Paul's Girls' School, Holst had the opportunity to become well acclamated with an environment where 125,000 people lived in an area just larger than three and one-half square miles. Hammersmith was a town of sharp contrasts, with the middle-class residing to the north, and the rest living near the poverty level around the shipyards, mills, and shops to the south along the bank of the River Thames.

Upon a cursory inspection of the title page in the full score, one will notice Holst's dedication *To the Author of "The Water Gypsies"* engraved just above the title line. The author, Sir Alan Patrick Herbert, was a contemporary of Holst who wrote a 414 page novel entitled *The Water Gipsies* in 1930, the same year that Holst composed *Hammersmith*. This novel explores the two worlds of Hammersmith through the character of a working-class girl caught in a love triangle between what has been described as an "illiterate river bargee and with a painter of aristocratic birth for whom she models. The local colour of Hammersmith is vividly described in the course of the narrative, but the author's central problem is to show his heroine's impossible attraction towards two different worlds so disparate that she can find no way to reconcile them."[2]

Holst accepted a position at Harvard University as lecturer in composition for the first six months of 1932. Meanwhile, Boosey & Hawkes made a decision to publish the military band version of *Hammersmith* and sent the score and parts to New York. "Oddly enough, it was partly because the original version of *Hammersmith* was in the United States the same time Holst was that the composer was contacted by Edwin Franko Goldman about conducting it on April 17, 1932, at the American Bandmasters' Association convention in Washington, D.C."[3]

In *Hammersmith*, Holst turns to the band to express musically a profound philosophic problem: the interplay between the humane and the mystical attitudes in a person's experience. This philosophic problem is the subject of a 1920 philosophical Essay by Gustav Holst entitled "The Mystic, the Philistine, and the Artist." The aloofness of the quiet River Thames is eloquently expressed in the opening section of the *Prelude*, which features a basso ostinato in F minor in the tuba and euphonium. Lasting just three measures, this basso ostinato is played a total of sixteen times before it begins to dissolve near the end of the *Prelude*.

Beginning in measure 4, Holst juxtaposes a "cantilena" in E major in the horn parts. Cantilena is here defined as an instrumental melody of lyrical character. This bi-tonal introduction sets the stage for the river, which is always the background to the crowd. *Hammersmith* is a study in paradoxes at many levels. Thinking in concert key, we find an opening statement with horns in 4 sharps, against tubas and euphoniums in 4 flats that add up to neither F minor, A-flat major, C-sharp minor, nor E major, not even at the cadences.

A visit to the Unites States Marine Band Library in Washington, D.C. in November of 1997 proved to be quite valuable in the author's personal journey to the source for more information on the premiere of *Hammersmith*. The records from rehearsals as well from the April 1932 performance indicate that although Holst was scheduled to conduct the premiere, he was unable to make the trip due to being hospitalized in Boston with an ulcer. The performance was conducted by Captain Taylor Branson, presumably from a two-line condensed score that was prepared by Donald Dixon, Librarian for the Marine Band.

As the years passed, the Marine Band performed *Hammersmith* on other occasions, and at least once under the baton of Frederick Fennell. Included in the Marine Band Library archives are copies from Fennell's "road copy" set of parts, which bear the following inscription on the title page: "Like the Thames it must move, [E Major over F Minor] however slowly: it must not be stagnant. Poco adagio, but a feeling—brooding, mysterious. A statement in which E Major over F Minor is more than convenient compositional juxtaposition."[4]

The decision to compose the Prelude in 4/2 meter came from what must have been Holst's desire for conductors and performers to understand the importance of and strictly adhere to the Poco adagio tempo marking at the beginning of the score. "Holst's obvious desire to harness the slowest pulse to the slowest-looking notation for the *Prelude* and to gain visual drive by casting the *Scherzo* in the familiar eights and sixteenths ought to work automatically—but it does not unless the conductor and the players really work at it."[5]

Even if one should decide not to program this work in a public concert, there is great benefit to both performers and conductor to sight-read, then rehearse the opening *Prelude* [measures 1–61] from *Hammersmith*. Holst has provided us with music that demands our utmost attention and focus on **not rushing**. A great laboratory experience is to set the opening tempo (half note at 60 beats per minutes suggested) with the metronome, then proceed to perform the opening *Prelude*, then check the final tempo (around measure 42) against the metronome to gauge consistency.

The *Scherzo* section of *Hammersmith* occupies the central portion of this one-movement work [measures 62–396] and provides artistic challenges of the highest order for everyone involved. During a visit with Frederick Fennell on 9 December 1997 he remarked to me that *Hammersmith* still represents some of the most treacherous stretches of music-making in all of the band's literature. Although not programmatic by definition, one can sense the noise, hustle, and exuberant vulgarity of the cockney crowd (from Imogen Holst's earlier quotation) in the *Scherzo*, which is developed from an opening motive used as a three-part invention found in measures 62–72.

Flutes [measures 62-68]

A second motive appears in 6/8 meter in the flute part beginning in measure 73, but is not prominently featured until measures 146–159, when Holst scores this motive in all of the wind parts.

Woodwinds [measures 146-160]

The third motive is introduced in the piccolo and E-flat clarinet parts beginning in measure 87 and is heard again in low brass from measures 110–114, but again is not featured prominently until cornets and trumpets double the upper woodwinds in measures 139–142.

Upper Winds + Cornets [measures 139-142]

The initial motive is presented again, but this time in augmentation in bassoons, euphoniums, and tubas from measures 160–165 against quartal harmonies in the rest of the brass section.

Bsns, Euph, Tuba [measures 160-165]

The short whistle of greeting, identified by Robert Cantrick as the "challenge theme" and first heard from the piccolo in the *Prelude* (measure 43) appears again in the *Scherzo*, this time in the cornets, then trumpets and trombones (measures 171–177), followed by an adaptation in the upper woodwinds (measures 177–180). This "challenge theme" appears several more times throughout the piece, most notably in thematic transformation (solo clarinet in measure 261 262), in the recapitulation of the *Scherzo* (oboe in measures 287 290), and in the climax of the *Scherzo* section (cornets and trumpets in measures 389–392).

Piccolo Solo [measures 43-44]

As the concluding section of *Hammersmith* returns to the three-measure basso ostinato, the River Prelude is now employed as a Postlude. The first motive from the *Scherzo* section is heard in successive entrances by solo woodwinds (E-flat clarinet in measures 400–402, oboe from measures 402–403, and alto and tenor saxophones in measures 403–405), while the "challenge theme" from the *Prelude* finds its way into the solo lines by the oboe (measures 397–398, and 407), in adaptation by the flute (measures 408–409), and in augmentation by the clarinet (measures 410–411). To this interesting contrapuntal texture, Holst introduces a return of the "cantilena" in measure 405, which eventually finds its way back to the horn parts which soar up to a concert C before melting away to a final statement in the trombones accompanied only by the basso ostinato in F minor in the tuba part which is finally reduced to a point where no feeling for a final cadence can be established. Perhaps, herein lay a paradoxical phenomenon—a work which neither falls apart nor falls together.

ENDNOTES

1. Imogen Holst, 2nd Rev. ed. *The Music of Gustav Holst* (London: Oxford University Press, 1968), 125.

2. Robert Cantrick. "Hammersmith and the Two Worlds of Gustav Holst." *Journal of Band Research* 12/2 (1977): 5.

3. Jon C. Mitchell. "The Premieres of Hammersmith." *College Band Directors National Association Journal* 2/2 (1984): 22.

4. Frederick Fennell, personal score to *Hammersmith.* Visit to U.S. Marine Band Library by author, 20 November 1997, Washington, D.C.

5. Frederick Fennell. "Gustav Holst's Hammersmith." Basic Band Repertory. *Instrumentalist* 31/10 (1977): 53.

A HOLST DISCOGRAPHY

Holst/Handel/Bach, Frederick Fennell and The Cleveland Symphonic Winds, (Telarc CD-80038), features performances of both of the Holst Suites for Military Band:

First Suite in E Flat, Op. 28, No. 1		
1.	Chaconne	4:37
2.	Intermezzo	2:48
3.	March	2:49
Second Suite in F, Op. 28, No. 2		
4.	March	4:22
5.	Song Without Words	2:40
6.	Song of the Blacksmith	1:20
7.	Fantasia on the "Dargason"	2:48

Holst, Dallas Wind Symphony, Howard Dunn (Reference Recordings RR-39CD), features performances of both of the Holst Suites, the Moorside Suite and Hammersmith:

	Suite #1 in E-Flat	10:21
1.	Chaconne	4:35
2.	Intermezzo	2:36
3.	March	4:10
	A Moorside Suite	13:58
4.	Scherzo	3:13
5.	Nocturne	6:35
6.	March	4:10
	Suite #2 in F	
7.	March	4:11
8.	Song Without Words	2:28
9.	Song of the Blacksmith	1:20
10.	Fantasia on the Dargason	3:14
11.	Hammersmith, Prelude and Scherzo	14:26

British and American Band Classics, Eastman Wind Ensemble, Frederick Fennell, (Mercury Living Presence, Philips Classics Productions, PolyGram Classics 432 009-2), features a performance of Hammersmith.

8.	"Hammersmith": Prelude and Scherzo, Op. 52	13:42

Tributes, North Texas Wind Symphony, Eugene Corporon, (Klavier KCD 11070), features a performance of Hammersmith.

9.	Hammersmith, Op. 52	13:25

Holst Series, Orchestral Works, London Symphony Orchestra, Richard Hickox, (Chandos CHAN 9420), features an orchestral performance of Hammersmith.

	Hammersmith, Op. 52	14:58
5.	Prelude: Poco adagio-	4:46
6.	Scherzo: Poco vivace	10:12

Bushes and Briars, Folksong Arrangements & Partsongs by Vaughan Williams, Holst, Elgar, Britten, Warlock, (EMI Classcis CMS 5 65123 2, USA CDMB 65123), features sixteen songs arranged by Holst including:

22.	The Song of the Blacksmith	1:16
25.	I Love My Love	4:04
26.	Swansea Town	2:51

These arrangements are performed by the Baccholian Singers of London, and provide a valuable resource for the wind band conductor desiring to hear the vocal interpretation of three folk songs used in Holst's Second Suite in F for Military Band.

Additional sources for recordings of the works of Holst include:

Holst, First Suite in E Flat, Kosei Wind Orchestra, (KOCD-2302)
Holst, First Suite in E Flat, Tokyo Kosei Wind Orchestra, (KOCD-3576)
Holst, First Suite in E Flat, Eastman Wind Ensemble, (SK 47198)
Holst, Hammersmith: Prelude & Scherzo, Kosei Wind Orchestra, (KOCD-3073)
Holst, Hammersmith: Prelude & Scherzo, Tokyo Kosei Wind Orchestra, (KOCD-3576)
Holst, Hammersmith: Prelude & Scherzo, Stockholm Wind Orchestra, (CAP 21415)
Holst, Second Suite in F, Kosei Wind Orchestra, (KOCD-2304)
Holst, Second Suite in F, Kosei Wind Orchestra, (KOCD-3563)
Holst, Second Suite in F, Tokyo Kosei Wind Orchestra, (KOCD-3576)

Ralph Vaughan Williams

CHAPTER
TWO

Ralph Vaughan Williams (b. Down Ampney, Gloucestershire, 12 October 1872; d. London, 26 August 1958) received his MusB at the Royal College of Music and studied with Bruch in Berlin (1897) and Ravel in Paris (1908). He shared many similar interests and ideals with Gustav Holst, whom he met at the RCM in 1895 and, like Holst, was overtaken by the folk song movement, which swept through England toward the close of the nineteenth century.[1] *In R.V.W.—A Biography of Ralph Vaughan Williams*, his wife, Ursula, wrote: "New arrangements were called for, piano accompaniments or choral settings; and because he knew and loved the music, Ralph was adept at providing them. Folk music weaves in and out of his work all through his life, sometimes adapted for some particular occasion, sometimes growing into the fabric of orchestral writing."[2] Vaughan Williams's commitment to the folk song movement can be seen by his participation first as a committee member for the Folk-Song Society (1909), later serving as one of several vice-presidents (1921), and finally his tenure as president of this organization in 1927.

English Folk Song Suite

Composed:	1923, Copyright 1924 by Boosey & Co., London.
First Performance:	4 July 1923 Royal Military School of Music at Kneller Hall.
Arrangement:	Orchestral version by Gordon Jacob, Copyright 1924 by Boosey & Co., London.
Important Note:	In order to made immediate comparisons between the vocal scores contained in this chapter and the full wind band score, it will be necessary to number all measures in the wind band score as this was never done by the publisher!

Vaughan Williams collected over 800 folk songs and used many of them in works he created throughout his career. Among his most famous is his *Fantasia on Greensleeves*, composed in 1934. **English Folk Song Suite** dates from 1923 and represents Vaughan Williams's first composition for wind band. A reviewer from *The Musical Times* commented, "The good composer has the ordinary monger of light music so hopelessly beaten." The piece was brought to prominence in this country by the 1957 Mercury recording of the Eastman Wind Ensemble, conducted by Frederick Fennell.[3]

This three-movement Suite opens with "March—Seventeen Come Sunday". Similar to the first movement of Holst's *Second Suite in F*, Vaughan Williams makes use of three tunes, the folk songs "I'm Seventeen Come Sunday" from measures 4–17, "Pretty Caroline" from measures 32–63, and "Dives and Lazarus" ("Diverus and Lazarus") from measures 64–96. In his third article on basic band repertory (*The Instrumentalist*, June 1976), Frederick Fennell states that Vaughan Williams probably found "Seventeen Come Sunday" from among the many notations by folk song collectors Cecil Sharp, Lucy Broadwood, and others. Research conducted at the Library of Congress in Washington, DC, reveals the primary source for "Seventeen Come Sunday" from Cecil Sharp's two-volume collection *English Folk Songs* (London: Novello & Co., 1921, Reprinted 1959). The version that most closely matches Vaughan Williams's treatment is the second of eight versions printed in Volume 1. An examination of the text reveals that a March tempo of 120 beats per minute would be appropriate for this movement.

The original is notated in E Dorian in 4/4 meter. Vaughan Williams adjusts the key to F Minor and makes use of the Dorian mode to notate the melody, this time set in 2/4 meter. Using diminished note values from the original, five subtle changes in the rhythm are noted as the main theme is stated in measures 5–17. The entire melody is repeated, this time scored as a tutti, leading into a two-bar transition.

At measure 32, we see the entrance of the next folk song, "Pretty Caroline." Vaughan Williams again went to Cecil Sharp's collection of English Folk Songs to use the second of three available versions.

The original, notated in D Major, was adjusted to A♭ Major for use in the Suite. Again, some subtle changes in the rhythm are noted, but the text can still be applied to the wind band lines in order to achieve a sense of phrase direction. A simple reading of this text helps to convey the sense of cantabile style needed to perform this section:

One morning in the month of May, How lovely shone the sun,
All on the banks of the daisies gay, There sat a lovely one.
She did appear as goddess fair, And her dark brown hair did shine.
It shaded her neck and bosom fair, Of my pretty Caroline.

Beginning in measure 64 a tune that was first thought to be originally composed by Vaughan Williams is introduced. Recent research by Richard Miles and his team of authors in *Teaching Music through Performance in Band* reveals this third tune as "Dives and Lazarus," used through measure 96 in the first movement.[4] Research in the collection **English Country Songs** (Lucy Broadwood, 1893) reveals a setting entitled "Lazarus," in which the name Diverus is also used throughout the text. The tune was noted by A. J. Hipkins, Esquire in Westminster and provided the material for Vaughan Williams to use with slight melodic and rhythmic adjustments.[5] The seven stanzas of text are a parallel to the biblical story found in Luke 16: 19–31. Although the story from the Bible never refers to the rich man by name, Dives is the Latin translation for rich man.[6]

The original in E Dorian was transposed to F Dorian to meet the obvious harmonic requirements of this contrasting middle section of the movement (the movement begins and ends in F Dorian). While the original is 24 measures in 4/4 meter, the last eight measures repeat both the melody as well as text from the previous eight-measure phrase. Given the first 16 measures of the original, we can see the transformation to 32 measures of 2/4 meter in the *English Folk Song Suite*. An analysis of the 71 notes used by Vaughan Williams in this section indicates that 34 of the notes represent an exact rhythmic match and 31 of the notes represent an exact melodic match.

Only 21 of the notes are an exact rhythmic as well as melodic match to the original, indicating that Vaughan Williams took certain liberties in this section to craft a presentation of a melodic line that would match the new countermelodic material presented in the upper woodwind voices. This point of view can be confirmed by reading the short program note found in the front of the 1940 Vaughan Williams score for string orchestra, *Five Variants of 'Dives and Lazarus'*, in which he states, "These variants are not exact replicas of traditional tunes, but rather reminiscences of various versions in my own collection and those of others."[7] Of the seven verses that comprise the text of "Lazarus," the following is perhaps the best syllabic match to the melodic idea as used by Vaughan Williams in this section:

So Lazarus laid him down and down,
Ev'n down at Diverus' door;
 "Some meat, some drink, brother Diverus,
Do bestow upon the poor."
"Thou art none of mine, brother Lazarus,
Lying begging at my door,
No meat, no drink will I give thee,
Nor bestow upon the poor."

The "Pretty Caroline" theme is heard once again from measures 97–129, then a *da capo* brings the piece back to "Seventeen Come Sunday" and a jump to a two-bar Coda which ends the movement in F Major.

The second movement titled **Intermezzo** consists of two folk songs, "My Bonny Boy" and "Green Bushes." In the condensed conductor's score, Vaughan Williams gives credit for the tune "My Bonny Boy" to Miss L. E. Broadwood from her collection titled *English County Songs*, and the Leadenhall Press.[8] This version represents the closest match to what Vaughan Williams used to begin his Intermezzo. The original key of D Dorian has been adjusted to F Minor (Dorian) for the wind band with subtle adjustments in the rhythm as seen in the previous tunes.

As is the case with many of these folk songs, we see evidence of certain measures in the original which have been lengthened (measures 12 and 17) to achieve a certain emotion from the vocalist. While Vaughan Williams did not depart from the 3/4 meter, his expression markings (measure 14 in the Suite) suggest that we might "stretch" here as well as when this same idea returns in measures 34 and 91. Also, an understanding of the words of this solemn song would assist any instrumental soloist in achieving the appropriate emotional character for the part.

I once loved a boy, a bonnie, bonnie boy,
I loved him, I'll vow and protest;
I loved him so well, and so very, very, well,
That I built him a berth on my breast,
That I built him a berth on my breast.

Beginning in measure 43, Vaughan Williams introduces the folk song "Green Bushes."

While credit was given to Miss L. E. Broadwood for the tune "My Bonny Boy" and later to Cecil Sharp for *Folk Songs from Somerset*, there is no mention on the title page of the condensed score about the use of "Green Bushes." Of the four versions printed in *Cecil Sharp's Collection of English Folk Songs, Vol. I*, version B most closely resembles Vaughan Williams's treatment. The original is notated in the Dorian mode with minor alterations to the rhythmic structure.

In another version taken from *One Hundred English Folksongs*, collected and arranged by Cecil J. Sharp, published by Oliver Ditson, Co. in 1916, we find an exact match in the modal structure of the melody to that of the wind band score, with only minor alterations to the melodic and rhythmic line. The alterations include: G and F eighth notes (measures 3, 7 and 15), G quarter note (measures 6 and 14), G and B♭ eighth notes (measure 8), B♭ quarter (measure 10), G, B♭, C, B♭, G, F eighths (measure 13), and C, B♭, F, E♭ eighths (measure 17).

While the wind score is marked *Poco Allegro (Scherzando)* beginning at measure 43, achieving the proper tempo can initially pose a problem. Although many conductors might simply prefer to imitate a tempo from a favorite recording, a closer look at the text can help to set an acceptable tempo for this section.

> As I was a walking one morning in Spring,
> For to hear the birds whistle and the nightingales sing,
> I sawed a young damsel, so sweetly sang she,
> Down by the green bushes she thinks to meet me.

As part of the score study and preparation process, singing the text from measures 43–58 in the wind score allows the conductor to determine not only the feel of the musical line, but to select an appropriate tempo as well.

While the close personal friendship which existed between Gustav Holst and Ralph Vaughan Williams is well documented, composer Percy Aldridge Grainger can only be indirectly linked by his own choices of English Folk Song settings. During 1905–06, Grainger scored a setting of "Green Bushes" for small orchestra with an arrangement for two pianos, six hands in 1919. Grainger states in his program notes: "Among country-side folksingers in England 'Green Bushes' was one of the best known of folksongs—and well it deserved to be, with its raciness, its fresh grace, its manly, clear-cut lines. The tune has also been noted in Ireland (see Nos. 368, 369, 370 of the Complete Petrie Collection) and in the United States (by Cecil J. Sharp, in the Southern Appalachian Mountains)."[9]

At measure 77, Vaughan Williams returns to the melody of "My Bonny Boy," this time with a different harmonic treatment. In listening to the London Symphony Orchestra recording of Gordon Jacob's arrangement of the *English Folk Song Suite*, recorded on 8 August 1970, one is struck by Sir Adrian Boult's interpretation of this section of the second movement where he emphasizes the harmonic lines, balancing them in such a way as to actually overtake the melodic line! In this orchestral recording, the differences in the harmonic treatment from measures 81–92 are brought out more clearly than in any band recording I have heard.[10]

A comparison of Vaughan Williams's wind band score to Jacob's orchestral score reveals more of a significant difference in scoring than in any other segment of the suite. Vaughan Williams scored the return of the "My Bonny Boy" melody in octaves between the Euphonium and Tuba, with the answer in Solo/1st Clarinet and 1st Cornet (melodically) and 2nd/3rd Clarinet and Cornet as well as Trumpets (harmonically). Jacob scored the return of the "My Bonny Boy" melody in octaves between the Cello and String Bass with the answer in 1st Clarinet (melodically) and Flute/2nd Clarinet (harmonically). This treatment places the flute part in the middle of the two clarinet parts, making for a most wonderful sonority not found when the same passage is scored for three clarinets doubled with two cornets and a trumpet in the band score.

Perhaps there is something to be gained here from the study of Gordon Jacob's orchestral arrangement; namely the possibility of a fresh sound in measures 81–92 by emphasizing both the 2nd Clarinet and 2nd Cornet parts in the wind band version. As with the final cadence in the first movement, Vaughan Williams once again employs the use of the Picardy third.

The third and final movement, "March—Folk Songs from Somerset" contains four different folk songs. The first, "Blow Away the Morning Dew," appears after a brief four-measure introduction in 2/4 meter. While Cecil Sharp's collection of English Folksongs was once again reviewed for source material, a version found in Cecil Sharp's *Folk Songs from Somerset* (London, 1904) reveals an arrangement of "Blow Away the Morning Dew" which is an exact match to the melody used in the wind band score.

With the exception of the original key of G Major adjusted to B♭ Major for the wind band version, a change of only three rhythms (measures 5, 6, and 15), one melodic note (measure 9) and one melodic addition (measure 12), everything else is similar between the vocal score and the wind band score. Again, knowledge of the text for this folk song helps to achieve the light style necessary for a stylistically correct interpretation.

Without any transition, Vaughan Williams immediately launches into "High Germany" beginning in measure 29 of the wind band score. The original in D Aeolian has been transposed to G Aeolian to keep continuity in the wind band score, with only two small melodic (measures 8 and 13) and two small rhythmic adjustments (measures 14 and 15) separating the original from Vaughan Williams's version for wind band. A further examination of the text of this folk song helps to establish a similar style of performance to that of "Blow Away the Morning Dew", which returns in measure 44.

O Pol - ly, Love, O Pol - ly, the rout has now be - gun And we must march a way at the beat-ing of the drum. Go dress your-self all in your best and come a - long with me, I'll take you to the cru - el wars in High Ger - man - ie.

After a two-bar transition (measure 69), the Trio begins, with a new melody introduced in the upper woodwinds at measure 73. The third folk song found in this movement is "The Tree So High." The primary source for this folk song has been difficult to locate. After comparing twelve different versions of this tune as well as others with a related title: "The Trees They Do Grow High," "Still Growing, or The Trees They Do Grow High," "The Trees They Are So High," "The Trees They Grow So High," no *exact* matches with the Vaughan Williams melody could be found.

In speaking with Malcolm Taylor, Head Librarian for the Ralph Vaughan Williams Memorial Library in London, England, some additional light was shed on this issue. Mr. Taylor felt that as Vaughan Williams titled the movement *Folksongs from Somerset*, the collections to search would be those of Cecil J. Sharp, as he was the only collector who traveled to Somerset to listen to the folksingers of that region.[11] Volume II of the *Journal of the Folk-Song Society* confirms that the ballad "The Trees They Do Grow High" was fairly well known in the "neighbourhood" of Langport, Somerset.[12] The following version from Cecil Sharp's Collection is the closest match that could be located. The similarities here are loosely found in the rhythm as well as the length of the tune.

The trees that do grow high And the leaves they do grow green; But the time is gone and past, my Lo - ve, that you and I have seen. It's a cold win - ter's night, my love, When you and I must bide a - lone. The bon - ny lad was young; but a grow - ing.

In his 1907 publication *English Folk Song: Some Conclusions*, Cecil Sharp offers the following information regarding variations of existing folk songs.

> Another frequent cause of variation arises when the singer, having partially forgotten his words, has substituted corrupt and unmetrical lines. The attempt to adapt the tune to these irregularities will often lead to the invention, unconscious of course, of interesting melodic changes. 'The Trees they do grow high', sung to me by Mr. Harry Richards of Curry Rivel, is an instance of this.[13]

Musical examples follow showing the same melody for the first eight bars with five different variations of the melody for the last eight bars! With so many versions of "The Trees They Do Grow High," one must conclude that Vaughan Williams must have used the variant that best suited his needs for measures 73–88.

The final folk song, "John Barleycorn," appears from measures 88–112 scored for the low brass. This is also an example of a folk song noted in many different versions. The closest match in a primary source for this tune was found in Volume III of the *Journal of the Folk-Song Society*.[14] Once again, while not a complete match to Vaughan Williams's treatment in the Suite, the ending (last two lines) of the original are an exact match to measures 105–112.

There was three men come from the North The vic - t'ry for to try Then these three men did vow and de - clare John Bar - ley - corn should die To my rite fol le rol lol lid - dle for le rol Rite fol le rol li day.

Based entirely on folk music sources, the three movements of Ralph Vaughan Williams's *English Folk Song Suite* provides us with references to nine different folk songs. Unlike the other works selected for this text, this work has offered the additional challenge of locating the variant of the folk song that most closely relates to the settings that Vaughan Williams used. Several of the nine folk songs gathered for this masterwork had anywhere from two to nine different variants. We have seen in this work how the words help to determine proper tempi as well as stylistic considerations for solo instruments as well as ensemble passages. As the themes from "Pretty Caroline," "My Bonny Boy," "Green Bushes," and "Blow Away The Morning Dew" are all played by instrumental soloists first, then followed by the ensemble, the soloists can glean a stylistically appropriate "model" from the vocalist's approach. In each case, singing the text to the written solo passage will create the opportunity for individual performers to become the music, which is one of several techniques that Barry Green uses in his Inner Game approach to letting go to the creative side of music-making. Green goes on to state, "Losing yourself in a character you are portraying musically, or in the emotions of the music, is another way of letting go."[15]

ENDNOTES

1. Stanley Sadie, ed., *The New Grove Dictionary of Music and Musicians,* vol. 19, *Ralph Vaughan Williams*, by Hugh Ottaway (London: MacMillan Publishers Limited, 1980), 569.

2. Ursula Vaughan Williams, *R.V.W.—A Biography of Ralph Vaughan Williams* (London: Oxford University Press, 1964), 151.

3. Captain Frank Byrne, United States Marine Band, program notes from "The President's Own" United States Marine Band Bicentennial Concert, John F. Kennedy Center for the Performing Arts, Washington, DC, 11 July 1998.

4. Richard Miles, ed., *Teaching Music Through Performance in Band* (Chicago: GIA Publications, Inc., 1997), 242.

5. Lucy E. Broadwood and J. A. Fuller Maitland, *English County Songs* (London: Leadenhall Press Ltd., 1893), 102–103.

6. Rev. Dr. Robert S. Norris of Westminster Presbyterian Church, interview by author, 30 June 1998, Upper St. Clair, PA.

7. Ralph Vaughan Williams, *Five Variants of 'Dives and Lazarus'* (London: Oxford University Press, 1940), i.

8. Lucy E. Broadwood and J. A. Fuller Maitland, *English County Songs* (London: Leadenhall Press Ltd., 1893), 146–147.

9. Percy Aldridge Grainger, *British Folk-Music Settings Nr. 25 Green Bushes Passacaglia for Two Pianos, Six Hands* (London: Schott & Co., 1921), i.

10. Boult, Sir Adrian, *Vaughan Williams*, EMI Classics CDM 7 64022 2, 1991, compact disc.

11. Head Librarian Malcolm Taylor of Vaughan Williams Memorial Library, phone interview by author, 18 June 1997, Library of Congress, Washington, D.C.

12. Cecil J Sharp, *Journal of The Folk Song Society*, vol. II (London: Baricott and Pearce, 1905–1906), 253.

13. Cecil J. Sharp, 4th rev. ed. Maud Karpeles, *English Folk Song: Some Conclusions* (Belmont, CA: Wadsworth Publishing Company, Inc., 1965), 32–34.

14. Lucy E. Broadwood, *Journal of The Folk Song Society*, vol. III (London: Baricott and Pearce, 1908–1909), 255.

15. Barry Green, *The Inner Game of Music* (New York: Doubleday, 1986), 94.

Sea Songs

Composed:	1923, Copyright 1924 by Boosey & Co., London.
Duration:	c. 4 minutes
First Performance:	April 1924 British Empire Exposition.
Transcription:	Orchestral version by the composer, 1942.
Important Note:	In order to made immediate comparisons between the vocal scores contained in this chapter and the full wind band score, it will be necessary to number all measures in the wind band score.

A 1923 review printed in the *Musical Times* of London reported on the first performance of the *English Folk Song Suite*, complete with a second movement entitled *Sea Songs*. Vaughan Williams eventually decided to remove it from the Suite and create a separate composition entitled *Sea* Songs, based on the folk songs "Princess Royal," "Admiral Benbow," and "Portsmouth."

This one-movement work, which is approximately four minutes in length, is very similar in overall design to the first movement of his *English Folk Song Suite*. Vaughan Williams begins with a four measure introduction, then presents three separate tunes, which include "Princess Royal" from measures 5–32, "Admiral Benbow" from measures 33–48, a return of "Princess Royal" from measures 49–71, and "Portsmouth" from measures 74–105. The *da capo* returns the listener to a repeat of both "Princess Royal" and "Admiral Benbow" before the work reaches the *fine* ending. When one considers the striking similarity between *Sea Songs* and "March—Seventeen come Sunday" from the *English Folk Song Suite*, it is easy to see why the decision was made to detach it from the original suite.

Sea Songs	March—Seventeen come Sunday
Intro [4 measures]	Intro [4 measures]
Princess Royal [28 measures]	Seventeen come Sunday [28 measures] (2 measure CODA)
Admiral Benbow [30 measures with repeat]	Pretty Caroline [32 measures]
Princess Royal [23 measures] FINE	Diverus & Lazrus [64 measures with repeat]
Trio [2 measure intro]	Pretty Caroline [32 measures] D.C.
Portsmouth [64 measures with repeat] D.C.	
Total = 229 measures	**Total = 192 measures**

The original melody of "Princess Royal" comes from a Morris Dance tune also known as "The Arethusa." Some confusion exists about the exact variant of the tune "Princess Royal," as there are numerous versions bearing the same title; unfortunately none of the melodies provide an exact note-for-note match to the material Vaughan Williams used for his first theme in *Sea Songs*. However, the first version found in Lionel Bacon's *Handbook of Morris Dances* (page 3), provides the match that must have been used by Vaughan Williams.

PRINCESS ROYAL (ABINGDON)

While the original was notated in the key of G Major, Vaughan Williams transposed it up one half step to A-flat Major for the wind band version and changed the meter from 4/4 to 2/4. He also made a slight melodic alteration in the first beat of the melody (measure 5 in the wind band score) and resolved the melody using a leading tone rather than the interval of a perfect fourth (measure 11) as seen in the original.

Set in the key in A-flat Major, the woodwinds (especially flute and piccolo) are featured prominently in the opening section. Although the tempo should be set by the material in the four measure introduction, there is often the tendency for the ensemble members playing the melody to slow down as they make the dynamic change from *ff* in the opening four measures to *p* when "Princess Royal" begins. The eighth-note staccato accompaniment from measures 5–19 should serve as a guide for those playing the melody, and it is important that they listen for how their melodic line fits to the accompaniment. There should be no change of tempo in measure 13 even though the dynamic suddenly changes to *ff*.

Beginning in measure 21, Vaughan Williams uses the second half of the tune from "Princess Royal," again with some slight alterations in the contour of the melodic line. This version is taken from the same variant of Lionel Bacon's *Handbook of Morris Dances* (page 3) to illustrate the original material from which Vaughan Williams worked.

PRINCESS ROYAL (B SECTION)

While Vaughan Williams uses the first four measures of the tune exactly as written, he departs in the four measures to compose something of his own design to maintain the rhythmic vitality of the phrase, making the same melodic alteration he did at measure 5 in the wind band score again at measure 29 before returning to the character of the original melody to end the phrase. Once again, the choice was made to use the leading tone for the melody in moving from measure 31 to 32 instead of the perfect fourth as notated in the original. The tune comes to a final cadence on A-flat in measure 32 and moves directly into C minor as the next folk song is unveiled.

While initial research conducted at the Library of Congress in Washington, DC, reveals one source for "Admiral Benbow" from Cecil Sharp's collection *One Hundred English Folk Songs* (Boston: Oliver Ditson Company, 1916), an examination of the wind band arrangement reveals that Cecil Sharp's melody is not close enough to qualify this variant as the match. The text, however, is very close to the correct variant of the tune. The real problem is that Vaughan Williams did not label his melody correctly; "Admiral Benbow" is actually "Benbow, The Brother Tar's Song." In 1859, William Chappell published a two-volume set entitled *Popular Music of the Olden Time* which contains "Benbow, The Brother Tar's Song." To our delight, we discover a melody which is an exact match for measures 33–48 of the wind band score, with the minor exception of the note on the downbeat of the second measure.

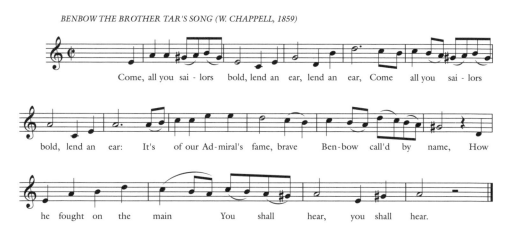

BENBOW THE BROTHER TAR'S SONG (W. CHAPPELL, 1859)

"Admiral Benbow was referred to as "the brother tar" because he rose from being a common sailor to the rank of Admiral. His father was Colonel John Benbow, a Shropshire gentleman and loyal Cavalier, who distinguished himself at the battle of Worcester, and was there taken prisoner. At the Restoration he could obtain no better post than one of subordinate rank in the Tower of London at a salary of eighty pounds a year, and left his family penniless. Portraits of Admiral Benbow may be seen at Hampton Court Palace and in the town-hall at Shrewsbury."[1]

The original folk song is notated in A minor, however Vaughan Williams chose to use this folk song to provide contrast, and scored it in C minor in the wind band version. After two phrases which are repeated in the form of a first and second ending, Vaughan Williams moves from the final cadence in C minor (measure 48) right back into A-flat Major for the repeat of the "Princes Royal" theme. Much has been written over the years about the harmonic language of composer Richard Strauss, especially in his use of chromatic third relations or chromatic mediants. An analysis of the Strauss *Allerseelen, Op. 10, No.8* for wind band reveals a string of these chromatic third relationships as the key center changes every four measures in the development section (measures 65–87) and passes through C minor, E♭ Major, G Major, B♭ minor, G minor, D Major, and B♭ Major (as a dominant seventh) on its way to resolving to E♭ Major in measure 91, marking the recapitulation. While nowhere near as elaborate as the Strauss example, the fact that Vaughan Williams used the chromatic third relationship to move from measures 32 to 33, and again from measures 48 to 49 demonstrates his fluency with the technique. A three measure phrase extension (measures 69–71) brings the repeat of the "Princess Royal" section to a close on an A♭ Major chord.

A two measure introduction to the Trio follows, modulating to D-flat Major and introducing the third folk song, "Portsmouth" from measures 74–106. The melody is marked *cantabile* and invites the conductor to use a slightly slower tempo to match the style of this melody as Vaughan Williams presents it in the context of this wind band masterwork. There is no indication for a tempo change or even the suggestion of a slower tempo in the part of Vaughan Williams, however, many conductors enjoy the opportunity to present lyrical themes at a slightly slower pace to allow maximum variety for the listener. The tune "Portsmouth" also has versions known as "The Parting." Again, an exact melodic match could not be located until comparing the version found in William Chappell's 1859 publication of *Popular Music of the Olden Time*. This version contains three stanzas of text as well as a performance indication of *Moderate time, and with expression*. Clearly, Vaughan Williams used this version as his source material for "Portsmouth."

The words to the tune "Portsmouth" are credited to Mr. John Oxenford. Constructed in the style of a ballad, the words suggest the story of a sailor parting with his love at Portsmouth. The tune, however, is much older and appears as a dance tune in John Playford's *English Dancing Master* of 1651. In order to achieve the original dance feel of this tune, one would have to sing (or play) it twice as fast as it appears in the Vaughan Williams score. Such is the life of great melodies, as they surface again and again, sometimes century after century.

A *da capo* returns us to the introduction of *Sea Songs*, and the reprise of the Morris Dance tune "Princess Royal," and "Benbow, the Brother Tar's Song" as a three measure phrase extension (measures 69–71) brings this gem of a wind band masterwork to a close.

After the first performance of the *English Folk Song Suite* on 4 July 1923, *The Musical Times* reviewed the concert and commented, 'The good composer has the ordinary monger of the light stuff so hopelessly beaten.' "This had been one of the works he had been particularly happy to undertake, as he enjoyed working in a medium new to him. A military band was a change from an orchestra, and in his not-so-far-off army days he had heard enough of the 'ordinary monger's light stuff' to feel that a chance to play real tunes would be an agreeable and salutary experience for bandsmen."[2] Though perhaps not as popular as the *English Folk Song Suite*, the *Sea Songs* of Vaughan Williams nevertheless deserves equal podium time as it was crafted from the same quality stock of creative effort.

ENDNOTES

1. William Chappell, *Popular Music in the Olden Time* (New York: Dover Publications, 1965), 678.

2. Ursula Vaughan Williams, *R.V.W. A Biography of Ralph Vaughan Williams* (New York: Oxford University Press, 1964), 152.

Toccata Marziale

Composed:	1924, Copyright 1924 by Boosey & Co., London.
Duration:	c. 5 minutes
First Performance:	1924 Royal Military School of Music Band conducted by Lt. H. E. Adkins at Wembley Stadium, London as part of the British Empire Exposition.
Important Note:	As there has not been a new critical edition of a full score and set of parts published since the original 1924 set, conductors should refer to Frederick Fennell's article in the August 1976 edition of the *Instrumentalist* for the list of the (40) corrections needed in the score and parts.

Similar to Holst's *Hammersmith*, the *Toccata Marziale* of Ralph Vaughan Williams represents another contrapuntal British wind band masterwork that should be rehearsed and hopefully programmed by wind band conductors. Although completed some six years before Holst's *Hammersmith*, it is easy to connect the interests of both composers in the engagement of a composition that would ultimately turn out to be an eloquent demonstration of compositional prowess involving contrapuntal writing. There are two excellent books about the life and music of Ralph Vaughan Williams, *R.V.W. A Biography of Ralph Vaughan Williams* by his wife, Ursula Vaughan Williams, and a companion book, *The Works of Ralph Vaughan Williams* by Michael Kennedy. Both were published in 1964 by Oxford University Press; unfortunately neither book makes any mention of the *Toccata Marziale*. In his article on the *Toccata Marziale*, Frederick Fennell recalls having the opportunity to meet very briefly with Vaughan Williams after a series of lectures in 1954 at Cornell University (Vaughan Williams' last visit to the United States before his death), but admits that the time was spent discussing *Folk Song Suite* and *Toccata Marziale*, but not about its origin. So, the exact origin of *Toccata Marziale* remains an unanswered question.

An interview with James F. Keene, Director of Bands at the University of Illinois, reveals a copy of a manuscript score by Ralph Vaughan Williams bearing the original title *Toccata in B-flat* as part of the archives in the University of Illinois Band Library. Clearly, this score is *Toccata Marziale*, thus connecting one more link to the unanswered question of the work's origin.[1]

As with the most effective performances of chamber music, it is necessary to develop a plan for how the piece will be balanced at all times. As we know, this process takes hours for mature chamber musicians who are not only fully engaged during rehearsals but also possess a great deal of experience in the balancing of parts within their performing ensemble. In order to effectively rehearse and perform *Toccata Marziale*, it will be necessary to present a master sheet to all of the musicians so that they can mark (at least) the principal lines when they occur in each individual part.

A suggestion for wind band conductors is to purchase an additional score which will be used for study and rehearsal purposes. After numbering all of the measures in the score, use highlighting crayons (the ones used to highlight a bible or other book with thin delicate pages), and mark the score as follows:

- Yellow indicates principal thematic material
- Green indicates countermelodic material
- Orange indicates thematic fragments that appear in canonic imitation
- Blue indicates additional fragments appearing in canonic imitation

The choice of color is certainly up to the individual conductor, but four colors will be needed to complete the study version of this score. Similar to our experiences as young students when first encountering the famous *Norton* scores, this highlighting helps to visually identify prominent material as well as allowing for immediate isolation of similar parts during rehearsal. Please refrain from using the common ink highlighters as they will bleed through the page and create a rather unpleasant finished product!

The following is a detailed list of each instrument part, and the appropriate measures to be highlighted (in yellow) in the conductor's score as well as marked in brackets in each performer's part. A pencil such as *Col-erase #20045* in Carmine Red is a favorite choice among professional studio musicians for part marking. (The *Col-erase #20060* in Indigo Blue and *Col-erase #20052* in Light Green are two other favorites for those desiring to mark study scores for rapid identification.)

Principal Thematic Material—Be sure to include any anacrusis or resolution. Some of the themes begin on either the first half or the last half of the measure as indicated.

Flute/Piccolo—12–13, 15–20, 30–40, 44–47, 62–73, 78–88, 93–95, 112 (last half), 114 (last half), 116–120, 124–134, 139–146.

E-flat Clarinet—12–13, 15–20, 30–40, 44–47, 57–73, 78–88, 112 (last half), 114 (last half), 116–120, 124–134, 139–146.

Oboes—12–13, 19–26, 34–40, 44–47, 51–53, 57–73, 85–91, 93–95, 112 (last half), 114 (last half), 128–134, 138–146.

Solo Clarinet—11–20, 30–32, 44–47, 65–67, 70–71, 78–84, 87–90, 93–95, 112 (last half), 114 (last half), 116–119, 124–126, 139–146.

1st Clarinet—9–20, 30–32, 44–47, 69–71, 73–74, 79–91, 93–95, 112 (last half), 114 (last half), 116–120, 124–126, 139–146.

2nd Clarinet—9–20, 35–37, 44–47, 67–68, 70–71, 73–74, 87–91, 93–95, 112 (last half), 114 (last half), 116–120, 129–131, 138–146.

3rd Clarinet—20, 30–32, 35–37, 47, 54–60, 70–71, 96–97, 101–102, 112 (last half), 114 (last half), 124–126, 129–131, 144–146.

Alto Clarinet—1–8, 13 (last half)–20, 53–57, 69, 71–72, 78 (last half)–82, 95–97, 102–102, 112 (last half), 114 (last half), 116 (last half).

Bass Clarinet—1–8, 19–22 (first half), 61–64, 75–82, 103–107, 112–113, 115, 120 (last half)–123.

Soprano Sax—4–8, 11–15, 20, 30–32, 35–40, 62–64, 69, 71–72, 97–103, 114 (last half), 116 (last half)–120 (first half), 128–134.

Alto Sax—1–8, 13 (last half)–18, 20, 53–57, 78 (last half)–82, 95–97, 101–102, 112 (last half), 114 (last half), 116 (last half).

Tenor Sax—1–4, 19–22 (first half), 61–64, 75–77, 78–82, 103–107, 112–113, 115 (first half), 120 (last half)–123.

Baritone Sax—1–4, 20 (last half)–22 (first half), 40–43, 48–51, 61–64, 103–107, 112–113, 115, 120 (last half)–123, 134–138, 149–152.

Bass Sax/Contra Bass Clarinet—1–4, 20 (last half)–22 (first half), 32–34, 41–43, 48–51, 75–78, 82–85, 90–93, 103–105, 112–113, 115 (first half), 120 (last half)–123, 126–128, 135–138, 147–153.

Bassoons—1–4, 20 (last half)–21, 32 (last half)–34, 61–64, 78 (last half)–84, 112–113, 115 (first half), 120 (last half)–123, 126 (last half)–128.

Horns—5–8, 19 (last half)–20 (first half), 34 (last half)–37, 46–47, (Hns.1–2) 51–52, (Hn. 2) 53–55, (Hns. 3–4) 60–63, (all) 95–102, 109–111, 114–115 (first half), 128–131.

Solo & 1st Cornet—4–15, 20 (last half)–21, (solo marked from 22–26 generally played by oboe), 34–40, 51–54, 57–61, 62–68, 70–71, 73–74, 93–101 (first half), 109–111, 113 (last half)–120 (first half), 128–134, 143 (last half)–146.

2nd Cornet—4–15, 20 (last half)–21, 34–40, 46 (last half)–47, 51–53, 57–61, 62–65, 70–71, 97–100, 109–111, 114 (first half), 115 (last half), 116 (last half)–120 (first half), 128–134, 143–146.

Trumpets—4–15, 34–40, 46 (last half)–47, 51–53, 68, 73–74, 97–100, 109 (last half)–111, 114 (last half)–115, 116 (last half)–120 (first half), 128–134, 143–146, 149–150.

Trombones—5–9, 20 (last half)–22 (first half), 26–30, (Bs. Tbn.) 32–34, (Tbns. 1–2) 34–38, (Bs. Tbn.) 41–43, (Tbns. 1–2) 46 (last half), (Bs. Tbn.) 48–51, (all) 60–64, (Bs. Tbn.) 77–78, (Tbns. 1–2) 93–96, (Tbn. 1) 101–102, (Bs. Tbn.) 103–108, (Tbns. 1–2) 106–111, (Bs. Tbn.) 112–113, and 115 (first half), (Tbns. 1–2) 113 (last half)–114 (first half), (all) 120 (last half)–124, (Bs. Tbn.) 126–128, (Tbns. 1–2) 128–132, (Bs. Tbn.) 134–137, and 149–152, (Tbns. 1–2) 150–152.

Euphonium—1–8, 19–21, 26 (last half)–30, 32–34, 41–43, 48–51, 53–57, 75–78, 90–94, 97–99, 103–106, 108–113, 115 (first half), 120 (last half)–124, 126–128, 135–138, 149–152.

Basses—1–4, 20 (last half)–23, 32–34, 41–43, 48–51, 75–78, 90–93, 103–105, 113, 115, 120 (last half)–124, 126–128, 135–138, 147–152.

String Bass—1–4, 20 (last half)–23, 32–34, 41–43, 48–51, 75–78, 90–93, 103–105, 113, 115, 120 (last half)–124, 126–128, 135–138, 146–152.

Timpani—26–27, 34–35, 116–122, 128–129, 146–152.

Snare Drum—15–19, 29–30, 38–40, 46, (triangle) 69–73, (snare drum) 78–82.

Countermelodic Material—These phrases should be highlighted in green (or your secondary color of choice) on the study score. Be sure to include any anacrusis or resolution. Some of the countermelodies begin on either the first half or the last half of the measure as indicated. Performers should bracket these measures in pencil to differentiate between principal thematic material and the countermelodies.

E-flat Clarinet—100–101.

Oboes—100–101.

1st Clarinet—100–101.

2nd Clarinet—100–101.

3rd Clarinet—12–14, 138–142.

Alto Clarinet—9–13 (first half), 138–142.

Bass Clarinet—9–14, 100–101.

Soprano Sax—138–142, 151 (last half)–152.

Alto Sax—9–13 (first half).

Tenor Sax—9–14, 100–101.

Baritone Sax—9–11.

Horns—151 (last half)–152.

Solo & 1st Cornet—138–142, 151 (last half)–152.

2nd Cornet—138–142, 151 (last half)–152.

Trumpets—151 (last half)–152.

Euphonium—9–14, 100–101.

Material that appears in Canonic Imitation—These fragments should be highlighted in orange (or your third color of choice) on the study score. Be sure to include any anacrusis or resolution. Some of the fragments begin on either the first half or the last half of the measure as indicated. Performers should use parenthesis to bracket these measures in pencil to differentiate between principal thematic material, countermelodies, and fragments used in canon.

Flute/Piccolo—43, 137.

E-flat Clarinet—41–43, 135–137.

Oboes—41–43, 135–137.

Clarinets—41–43, 135–137, (Solo & 1st Cl.) 147, (2nd & 3rd Cl.) 147 (first half).

Soprano Sax—41–43, 135–137.

Solo & 1st Cornets—41–43, 135–137, 147–148.

2nd Cornet—147–148.

Trombones—147–148.

Euphonium—147–148.

Additional Material that appears in Canonic Imitation—These fragments should be highlighted in blue (or your fourth color of choice) on the study score. Be sure to include any anacrusis or resolution. One of the fragments begins on the first half of the measure as indicated. Performers should also use parenthesis to bracket these measures in pencil to differentiate between principal thematic material, countermelodies, and other fragments used in canon.

Solo & 1st Cornet—149.

2nd Cornet—41–43, 135–137.

Trumpets—41–43, 135–138, 147–148.

Bass Trombone—147–148.

As one can see, there is a significant amount of time spent to simply prepare the study score for rehearsal as well as additional time on the part of the performers (away from rehearsal) to mark their parts for identification. However, the beauty of this preparation can be immediately realized during the first rehearsal when various lines (marked at the same dynamic level) will be balanced in such a manner to produce the desired effect without having the wind band overplaying the parts. This method of highlighting the principal lines seems to work better for balancing *Toccata Marziale* than the usual practice of having those instruments playing the sustained sounds reduce their level. Obviously, the ground rules for effective chamber music come into play; one does not play a line marked *forte* with quite the same emphasis if it is not a principal line. When counterlines are being played, one must effectively balance with the principal line. Generally speaking, if the performer playing the counterline is able hear the principal line, balances should be very close to being correct. And, all parts that are not included in some sort of bracket are somewhat less important at that moment; therefore, they should be played with a bit less volume.

Once the performers understand their role in the piece (and the roles change quite a bit), they are on their way to a much more informed interpretation. This, of course, can lead to a cleaner, more precise performance in which the performers maintain effective balances throughout the composition without overplaying material that simply gets in the way of the fundamental musical ideas within the composition. There are, however, a few dynamic indications that one may wish to adjust to improve overall balances, which are noted as follows:

• Consider reducing the dynamic markings in the horns, cornets, and trumpets at measure 48 down to *forte,*
• Consider increasing the dynamic markings in the contra bass clarinet and bassoon parts at measure 53 up to *mezzo piano,*
• Insist on *forte marcato* from the Solo & 1st Cornets at measure 67,
• Consider increasing the dynamic markings in the trombone and euphonium parts at measure 84 up to *mezzo piano,*
• Consider the addition of an eighth note on "G" in the timpani part in measure

106 to match the upper octave of the tuba (or euphonium) part. If this note can be embellished by adding two grace notes (looks like a three-stroke ruff or drag rudiment for percussionists), it really solidifies the harmonic change to G minor in this measure.

- Consider reducing the dynamic markings in the cornets at measure 138 down to *mezzo piano*,
- Consider rewriting the timpani part from measures 147–152 to Gb/Ab eighth notes to support the bass line, and
- Consider suggesting that the performers change dynamics from *fff* in measure 156 down to *mp* in measure 157 to effectively set the crescendo that ends the piece.

This is also a wonderful composition to use as a project to lead students to an understanding of the creative process used by a composer. In the case of *Toccata Marziale*, Vaughan Williams creates a 158 measure composition based on a single motive that is developed both melodically and rhythmically in five additional musical ideas (diagrammed as themes) derived from the original motive. The score to *Toccata Marziale* can be diagramed according to the following structure:

A Theme: Main Motive 1–4, (modified) 5–8, (modified) 48–51, (modified) 51–53, 91–94, 96–97.

[measures 1-4]

B Theme: 9–15.

[measures 9-15]

C Theme: 15–22.

D Theme: 22–26, (modified) 26–30, (modified) 30–32, (rhythmic modification) 32–34, (return of D) 116–120, 128–131.

E Theme: 54–60, (modified) 61–68, 93–95, 97 105, 106–110.

F Theme: 69 74.

Of particular interest is the ability of Vaughan Williams to use the different modifications of the motives (diagrammed here as themes) either dovetailing into one another or layered over top of each other:

A Theme 91–93 with E Theme 93–95, then

A Theme 96–98 with E Theme 97–105 a as well as B Theme 100–104

C Theme (end) 108–111 with E Theme 106–110

Note how the material from measures 44–47 is expanded when it returns later in the composition 138–146.

While the key signature of B-flat major is used throughout the piece, Vaughan Williams is able to adjust the key center as the work progresses through the use of accidentals allowing him to move to the tonality of G-flat major (measure 91), and back to B-flat major (measure 117). A most interesting chord progression from measures 144–146 (B♭, A♭7, F7, E♭, D♭7, E♭, Fmi7, G♭) allows Vaughan Williams to arrive at the coda in G-flat major and building to the final chords of G♭, B♭, C to arrive back in B-flat major to end the composition.

In his August 1976 *Instrumentalist* article on Basic Band Repertory and the Vaughan Williams *Toccata Marziale*, Frederick Fennell had this to say about the strangely infrequent performances of this work. "We conductors who shy away from demanding contrapuntal works of this dimension are probably to blame for such infrequent performances. But today the contrapuntal experience is sought out by so many young players who are eager to come to grips with this sort of intellectual and musical complexity. We are denying them a vital experience by avoiding such music, just because it may not play with ease…at first. The *Toccata* is difficult rhythmically, not because of complex or diverse meters, but in the sophisticated placement of simple fundamental rhythmic impulses and in the constant demand for vitality of tonal production in their precise execution."[2] Reading this article by Frederick Fennell, and then subsequently studying the score in greater depth each time I would prepare this work to teach and perform over a twenty-year period is what finally helped me to understand what is considered to be the most significant work Ralph Vaughan Williams ever composed for wind band. This composition is worth every ounce of creative energy and risk that you invest in its teaching and performance.

ENDNOTES

1. James F. Keene of University of Illinois, interview by author, 28 December, 2004, Champaign, IL.

2. Frederick Fennell, "Vaughan Williams Toccata Marziale." *The Instrumentalist* 31/1 (1976): 50.

A VAUGHAN WILLIAMS DISCOGRAPHY

Stars and Stripes, Frederick Fennell and The Cleveland Symphonic Winds, (Telarc CD-80099), features performances of Sea Songs, and the English Folk Song Suite.

10.	Sea Songs	4:01
	Folk Song Suite	
12.	March: Seventeen Come Sunday	3:19
13.	Intermezzo: My Bonny Boy	3:43
14.	March: Folk Songs from Somerset	3:32

Vaughan Williams, Serenade to Music, (EMI Classics CDM 7 64022 2), contains Gordon Jacob's orchestration of the Vaughan Williams English Folk Song Suite, featuring the London Symphony Orchestra, Sir Adrian Bolt conducting.

	English Folk Song Suite (arr. Gordon Jacob)	
2.	March (Seventeen Come Sunday)	2:54
3.	Intermezzo (My Bonny Boy)	2:52
4.	March (Folk Songs from Somerset)	2:59

Additional sources for recordings of the works of Vaughan Williams include:

Vaughan Williams, English Folk Song Suite, Kosei Wind Orchestra, (KOCD-3563)
Vaughan Williams, Toccata Marziale, Eastman Wind Ensemble, (MK 44916)
Vaughan Williams, Toccata Marziale, Kosei Wind Orchestra, (KOCD-3576)
Vaughan Williams, Toccata Marziale, Kosei Wind Orchestra, (KOCD-2811)

Percy Aldridge Grainger

CHAPTER
THREE

PERCY ALDRIDGE GRAINGER (b. 8 July 1882 Melbourne, Australia; d. 20 February 1961 White Plains, NY), pianist, composer, folksong collector, writer, teacher, and conductor, spent his childhood years in his homeland where he studied piano with Louis Pabst. Grainger moved to Germany in his teens along with his mother, and continued his studies at the Hoch Conservatory in Frankfurt from 1895–99. By 1901 Grainger had settled in England as a successful concert pianist, a profession which would support his two greatest loves—collecting folk songs and composing. As an avid collector of English, Danish, Norwegian and Australian folk songs, Grainger began in 1905–06 to collect folk songs in the English countryside using the newly invented wax cylinder phonograph. In the four years that followed, Grainger collected, recorded and transcribed approximately 300 British folk songs and assembled a collection of 216 Edison cylinders.[1] He later drew upon this collection of source material for his series of British folk-music settings for chorus, band, orchestra as well as various other combinations of instruments and voices. This emergence as a leading folk song collector of his day earned him a position among such leading composers as Holst and Vaughan Williams.

Grainger's output as a composer included a number of works that were either originally composed for wind band or eventually set for wind band. Since Grainger was famous for working on projects over a period of time as well as continuing to revisit and revise his works, we are left with a most interesting array of composition dates as well as subsequent revisions as the following list demonstrates:

Children's March "Over the Hills and Far Away" (1916–1918 for piano, military band)
    An original work for band even though the tunes sound like folk songs
    Military Band version published in 1919 by Schirmer

Colonial Song (1911 for piano as a "Yule gift" to his mother, Rose Grainger)
     "Elastic" scoring edition for theatre band in 1911–12
     Military Band version published in 1921 by Carl Fischer

Country Gardens (1908–1918)
     Version for band in 1931
     Orchestration in 1949–50 at the request of Leopold Stokowski for a 1951
     recording, which included seven works by Grainger

English Waltz from the *Youthful Suite* for Orchestra
     (Scored between 1899–1901, revised 1940–47)
     Transcribed for band in 1987 by David McKinney
     Edited by Mark Rogers in 1999 and published by Southern Music Company

Hill Song No. 1 (1901 for 2 piccolos, 6 oboes, 6 cor anglais, 6 bassoons and contra-
     bassoon)
     Rescored in 1921 for a more conventional wind group
     Published in 1922 by Universal Edition

Hill Song No. 2 (written in1907 for a solo wind ensemble of 23 to 24 instruments
     & cymbal)
     A personal favorite of Grainger's, dedicated to his friend Henry Balfour Gardiner
     Revised in 1911, rescored the work in 1929
     Published in 1950 by Leeds Music / Reprinted by TRN Music Publishers
     (undated)

Irish Tune from County Derry (1902–1911)
     Scored for Military Band from 1902–1911
     No. 20 of British Folk Music Settings
     Published in 1918 by Carl Fischer
     Published in 1937 by Schott/Schirmer
     Orchestration in 1949–50 at the request of Leopold Stokowski for a 1951
     recording, which included seven works by Grainger

Lincolnshire Posy (1905–1937)
     Considered by many to be his finest achievement in wind band writing
     Commissioned for American Bandmasters Association 1937 convention in
     Milwaukee
     Scored for Military Band in 1937
     No. 34 of British Folk Music Settings
     Published in 1940 by Schott/Schirmer
     Published in 1987 by Ludwig Music (Frederick Fennell's critical edition)

Molly on the Shore (Original setting for String Quartet as a "birthday gift" to his
     mother in 1907)
     Based on two Cork reels from *The Petrie Collection of the Ancient Music of Ireland*.
     Scored for Military Band in 1920
     No. 23 of British Folk Music Settings
     Published in 1921 by Carl Fischer, new critical edition published in 2002

Shepherd's Hey! (Setting of an English Morris tune given to Grainger in 1908 by
     Cecil Sharp)
     Scored for Military Band in 1918
     No. 21 of British Folk Music Settings
     Published in 1918 by Carl Fischer

The 'Gum-Suckers' March (Originally 'Cornstalks' March) (1905–1914)
     The only movement from the orchestral Suite *In a Nutshell* transcribed for
     Band in 1942

The Lads of Wamphray March (1905, revised 1937)
     Premiered on the same program as *Lincolnshire Posy* at the
     American Bandmasters Association 1937 convention in Milwaukee
     Published in 1941 by Carl Fischer

The Power of Rome and the Christian Heart (1913–1943)
     Commissioned by the League of Composers for Edwin Franko Goldman's
     70th birthday.
     Grainger's longest and most ambitious work for band, scored for large wind
     band, organ, keyboards, 'tuneful percussion' and optional strings.
     Published in1953 by Mills Music

Ye Banks and Braes O' Bonnie Doon (1901)
     Based on the traditional Scottish melody *The Caledonian Hunt's Delight*
     First scored for Military Band in 1918, Revised c. 1932
     No. 32 of British Folk Music Settings
     Published in 1937 by Schott
     Published in 1949 by Schirmer

It is no small coincidence that Percy Grainger's brilliant writing for wind band
was influenced directly by his service as a bandsman of the 15th Band of the Coast
Guard Artillery Corps, located at Fort Hamilton in South Brooklyn. Grainger, along
with his mother, had relocated to New York City in September 1915, and he was
busy performing as a concert artist when President Woodrow Wilson declared war in
Germany on April 5, 1917. Within two months, Grainger had purchased a soprano
saxophone and enlisted as a bandsman. Grainger described the early part of his army
career as being some of the happiest days in his life. He had the time to study and
practice on various wind band instruments, compose daily, and even conduct the
band on a few occasions. His time with the band allowed him to experiment and
develop a unique style for wind band scoring, which is so evident in his wind band
compositions. Percy Grainger became an American citizen on June 13, 1918. "His
compositional output from this period shows a sensitive ear for wind sonorities such
as could have only come from a close association with these instruments. Both *Shepherd's Hey* and *Irish Tune from County Derry* emerged in arrangements for band and
are more than just skillful textbook examples of how to score for wind band; they
encompass, too, an ingenuity and bold innovation in choice and combination of
instrumental textures."[2]

As one can see, Percy Grainger embraced the wind band as viable ensemble for his music along with orchestra, chamber ensembles, and piano. The end of this chapter contains a fascinating discography documenting numerous recordings of Grainger's works. One company in particular, Chandos Records Ltd. of Colchester, Essex, England has made the commitment to record the entire body of works by Percy Grainger, which is expected to occupy twenty-five compact discs when completed.

While decisions regarding the repertoire to be included in this text for Holst and Vaughan Williams were obvious, a rather selective process was employed to arrive at the pieces to represent Percy Grainger in this chapter. There is no doubt that one of the most popular of the Grainger works set for band is *Irish Tune from County Derry*. Our profession is most grateful to Frank Battisti and Robert Garofalo for their wonderful text, *Guide to Score Study for the Wind Band Conductor* (published in 1990 by Meredith Music Publications), in which we find a most comprehensive example of score study and analysis using *Irish Tune from County Derry* (pages 36–53). Next, there were considerations regarding accessibility of the literature, availability of published versions for study and performance, and frequency of performance of Grainger's wind band literature.

Grainger's *Lincolnshire Posy* is central to the core study of this text; Grainger collected hundreds of folksongs and selected just five to represent "a bunch of musical wildflowers" as Grainger so eloquently phrased it. The fiddlin' nature of the two Cork reels that Grainger borrowed from *The Petrie Collection of the Ancient Music of Ireland* provides a virtuosic display for wind musicians as well as a delight for the audience in *Molly on the Shore*. And, the recent availability of a band version of Grainger's fifth movement from his *Youthful Suite for Orchestra* certainly merits attention as we are hearing more performances each year of the *English Waltz*.

Lincolnshire Posy

Collected:	1905–06 (first five songs noted down directly from their folksingers)
Composed:	1937, Copyright 1940 by G. Schirmer, Inc.
First Performance:	7 March 1937 Milwaukee, WI at the 8th Annual Convention of the American Bandmasters Association.
Revised Edition:	by Frederick Fennell 1987, published by Ludwig Music Publishing Co.

Lincolnshire Posy was conceived and scored by Grainger in 1937. He was most careful to give credit to both the source as well as the singer from whom he recorded each selection. This indebtedness is reflected most profoundly in the 1940 published score from G. Schirmer which contains five complete pages of notes as well as important information on the first page of each of the six movements. While Frederick Fennell's 1987 full score edition represents a long-awaited triumph in both musical scholarship and preparation of a definitive version of this work (the original had over 500 errors in both score and parts), access to the original 1940 compressed full score affords a conductor valuable insights into this masterwork, insights which should not be overlooked. "Indeed, Grainger's largest essay for winds, *Lincolnshire Posy*, is a handbook of band orchestration and arguably the most idiomatic and sensitive composition ever written for large wind ensemble."[3]

A fascinating account of the world premiere of Grainger's *Lincolnshire Posy* on 7 March 1937 is offered in an article by Mark Grauer, "Grainger's Lost Letters on Lincolnshire Posy."[4] While the exact details are not clear from the article, it seems as if Grauer was going through the personal effects of deceased Milwaukee band director Joseph Bergeim (1895–1968), when he discovered several pieces of correspondence from Gainger to Bergeim regarding the premiere of *Lincolnshire Posy*. The American Bandmasters Association commissioned Grainger in December 1936 to write two band works for a premiere at the 1937 convention, an event which was organized by Joseph Bergeim. Although called the Milwaukee Symphonic Band, the group was really sponsored by Local #8 of the Musicians Union, and was made up primarily of members from the Blatz Brewery American Legion Post. These players, unaccustomed to the complex harmonies and rhythms presented in two of the movements, made the rehearsal a difficult one for Grainger. Ultimately, the *Rufford Park Poachers* and *Lord Melbourne* movements were dropped from the program. Grainger later wrote that the band was ". . . keener on their beer than on the music."[5]

The first movement, *Dublin Bay* (Sailor's Song), now titled *Lisbon* (Sailor's Song) was collected under what Grainger describes as characteristic circumstances. He met Mr. Dean (also spelled Deane and Deene in various sources), of Hibbaldstowe in 1905 at Brigg, N. E. Lincolnshire. As Dean began to sing *Dublin Bay*, the poignant memories of this old song, which he had not sung for forty years, made him burst into tears. Grainger returned on 25 May 1908, this time with the wax cylinder phonograph, determined to note down this song, even as Dean lay in a hospital ward. Between the second and third verse he spoke these words into the record: "It's pleeazin' meh," demonstrating just how much folksinging was a part of the folksinger's natural life.[6]

For several years, the Library of Congress in Washington, D.C. housed the collection of Percy Grainger's manuscripts; they have since been returned to the Grainger Museum in Melbourne, Australia. The collection was, however, transferred to microfilm in 1979, which allows researchers the firsthand opportunity to view Grainger's work.

The first example from this microfilm collection is Grainger's manuscript sketch for a solo piano version of *Dublin Bay*, complete with fingerings and notes regarding the use of the middle pedal for sustained passages. When the left hand enters in measure 16, Grainger gives the stylistic marking, *jumpingly*.

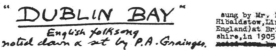

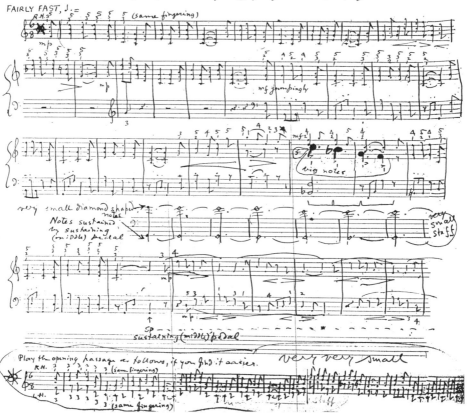

One will note the index card attached to the sketch, typed by Grainger, giving a full accounting of the circumstances surrounding this folk song. Perhaps it is from this primary source that the program notes in the 1940 edition of the wind band score were prepared.

In listening to a reproduction of the original cylinder recording as sung by Mr. Dean, it sounds as if he sang the four verses of *Dublin Bay* in E♭ Dorian, very close to a notated version of *Lisbon* in D Dorian found in Volume II of the *Journal of the*

Folk-Song Society.[7] When Grainger finally scored the piece for wind band, he chose A♭ Mixolydian, using the D♭ signature as a convenience.

The date of 24 September 1937 is found at the end of the next item, a piano score completed in the same year he scored the work for wind band. Although Grainger did correct the title on the piano score to read *Lisbon*, it was erroneously printed in the 1940 pubished score as *Dublin Bay*. Note that Grainger writes the word *heroicly* in his 1937 piano score: a clear indication of what his intentions were as well as what our intentions should be when interpreting this theme of the first movement.

An interesting footnote at the bottom of the page shows this heroic solo line to be a free adaptation of "The Duke of Marlborough," an English Folk Song collected by Miss Lucy E. Broadwood in 1895 from the singing of Henry Burstow of Horsham, Sussex.[8] Grainger used this folk song in 1939 as the basis for a short instrumental piece, *The Duke of Marlborough Fanfare*. This fanfare is used as the opening piece on Chandos Records ***The Grainger Edition, Volume One***, which includes a collection of eleven of Grainger's works for Orchestra and one for Symphonic wind band.[9]

The microfilm collection also reveals two additional sketches which clearly show Grainger's intent with regard to the wind band scoring; namely the "heroic" horn soli (measures 36–49) and the ending (measures 61–72). Interestingly, they bear the date of 19 June 1931; some six years before he actually set this work for wind band! Clearly, Percy Grainger had it in his mind to create an instrumental composition based on English Folk Songs long before the 1936 commission from the American Bandmasters' Association.

In researching the text for *Lisbon,* Volume II of the *Journal of the Folk-Song Society* contains a variant of the tune with text as sung by Mrs. Lock at Muchelney Ham in April, 1904.[10] (The tune actually bears a resemblance to "God Rest You, Merry Gentlemen!") Grainger chose to set four of the five verses as his first movement of *Lincolnshire Posy.*

One particular visit to the Folklife Reading Room in the Jefferson building of the Library of Congress proved to be most productive, as Archivist Jennifer Cutting shared two folders of information on Percy Grainger containing published as well as unpublished materials. The correspondence in these folders between the Library of Congress and the Grainger Museum in Melbourne, Australia reveals the chain of events leading to the preservation of the numerous wax cylinder recordings made by Grainger in the field just after the turn of the century. The Federal Cylinder Project was inagurated by the American Folklife Center in 1979 to locate, preserve, and document wax cylinders scattered throughout the collections of the Library of Congress, the Smithsonian Institution and other Federal Agencies. The Percy Grainger collection was accessioned by the Archive of Folk Culture with the assistance of Dr. Kay Dreyfus, Curator of the Grainger Museum. In a letter of 30 November 1981 to the American Folklife Center from Grainger Museum Assistant Curator Helen Reeves, she states:

> Yes, the Grainger Museum holds the original cylinders for the English folksong collection but most of those were ruined by fungus and are unplayable. Some

are in reasonable condition with only slight fungal damage, but others are completely ruined. However, we do have some acetate discs which were taken from the cylinders by the Library of Congress and I believe that Cecil Sharp House also has copies of Grainger's collection of English Folksongs.[11]

This same folder also includes a listing of all of the Grainger wax cylinders that were transferred to 7″ reel-to-reel tape format for preservation by the Library of Congress. What a thrill to peruse the seven page list, select a few representative folk songs, then go to the Madison building to actually hear the recorded sound of folk singers such as George Wray and Joseph Taylor (two of Grainger's favorite folk singers). Another interesting document located in the Grainger folder is a copy of the July, 1984 newsletter from the *International Association of Sound Archives*, containing a fifteen-page listing (tunes from *Lincolnshire Posy* are listed in appendix) of Grainger's cylinder collection from the Grainger Museum in Melbourne, Australia.

The second movement, *Horkstow Grange* (The Miser and his Man—a local Tragedy), was noted down by Grainger in 1905 from the singing of George Gouldthorpe of Goxhill, North Lincolnshire, England. Gouldthorpe's recording sounds as if it is in the key of A Major, while Grainger's scoring for wind band is in the key of D♭ Major. While reading the full lyric and recoiling at its horrors, it is obvious, according to Frederick Fennell, that Grainger chose to set it as a kind of requiem to both men and their "falling out" rather than to react creatively to the violence in the words. Grainger truly produces a completely non-violent and sonorous setting of this tune.[12]

As *Horkstow Grange* does not appear in any of the eight volumes of the *Journal of the Folk-Song Society* or in any of Cecil J. Sharp's collection of English folk songs, it becomes obvious that this particular song was context specific. It tells the story of a local tragedy (at a farm house on the road to South Ferriby, about eight miles north of Brigg), a tale of brutal violence against an oppressive overseer by his man who obviously couldn't take it any more. The liner notes on Percy Grainger's **Unto Brigg Fair** recording of 1908 (Leader LEA 4050) tell the story of John Bowling, a foreman on a farm at Horkstow and John "Steeleye" Span, a waggoner under Bowling's control. (Thus the term *him and his man* in line three should be understood as... his foreman.)

In Horkstow Grange there lived an old miser,
You all do know him as I've heard say.
It's him and his man (that was) named John Bowlin'
They fell out one market day.

Chorus Pity them who see him suffer,
        Pity poor old Steeleye Span;
        John Bowlin's deeds they will be remembered;
        Bowlin's deeds at Horkstow Grange.

With a blackthorn stick John Bowlin' struck him,
Oftens had threatened him before;
John Bowlin' turned round all in a passion,
He knocked old Steeleye onto t'floor.

        Pity them who see him suffer, [etc.]

John Bowlin' struck him quite sharply;
It happened to be on a market day,
Old Steeleye swore with all his vengeance,
He would swear his life away.

Pity them who see him suffer, [etc.][13]

Evidently, Grainger must have recorded George Gouldthorpe's singing a second time, as we see a sketch dated 28 July 1906 from Brigg, Lincolnshire, England. It is interesting to note the exacting rhythmic notation in the original, and how Grainger subsequently made adjustments in the meter of the wind band score to hold true to the performance practice of the folksinger. No other versions of this song are known and it does not appear to have been issued on broadsides (the generic term for a single unfolded sheet, usually folio size, containing texts printed on one side only) in the district or even in adjacent areas where printers were more active.[14]

One final thought regarding the erroneous title of *Harkstow Grange* in the 1940 wind band score should be discussed. An inspection of Grainger's handwriting (see previous musical example) shows the second and third letter connected (as in cursive handwriting), but the last four letters printed. Looking at the letter **a** in the word Grange (also written in cursive, but not connected), one would assume the first word to be Harkstow. This, among other instances, leads one to contemplate whether or not Grainger actually had the time to proofread the published compressed full score prior to the 1940 printing.

Rufford Park Poachers (Poaching Song) is the title of the third movement, and was sung on 4 August 1906 by Mr. Joseph Taylor, at Brigg, Lincolnshire who, according to Grainger, knew more folksongs than any of his other folksingers. Grainger "phonographed" this song and also "noted it down" exactly the way Joseph sang it, later publishing this song in Volume III of the *Journal of the Folk-Song Society*.[15]

Phonographed and noted by Percy
Grainger

According to Grainger, Joseph Taylor sang his songs with "purer" folksong traditions, neither illiterate or socially backward; and this fact is evident from Grainger's recording of Mr. Taylor. As Mr. Taylor sang different versions, Grainger must have been hard pressed to make a final decision for the wind band score. As a result, we have two possibilities for the opening fifty measures of *Rufford Park Poachers,* which differ from each other in key signature as well as orchestration.

Version A in the key of F Minor features a quartet of soloists including Piccolo, E♭ Clarinet, B♭ 1st Clarinet, and Bass Clarinet with a long Flügelhorn solo beginning with the anacrusis to measure 20. **Version B**, written in the key of C Minor, is orchestrated for a quartet including Piccolo, Oboe, Bassoon, and Alto Clarinet with a long Soprano Saxophone solo. Grainger expressed a preference for Version B.[16] With matters of key signatures and orchestration addressed, the most striking feature of *Rufford Park Poachers* is in the metric organization of the folk song itself, which includes the following form:

Original (Corresponds to the first 2 verses of text)
2/4, 5/8, 2/4, 5/8, 2/4, 5/8, 3/4, 2/4, 5/8, 3/4, 2/4, 3/4, 5/8, 2/4, 5/8,
     3/4, 5/8, 2/4, 5/8, 3/4, 2/4, 5/8, 2/4.

This original was then adapted rhythmically for wind band in the following manner:

Version A (Corresponds to the first 2 verses of text)
4/8, 5/8, 4/8, 5/8, 4/8, 5/8, 4/8, 5/8, 3/4, 5/8, 2/4, 3/8, 5/8, 3/4, 3/8,
     2/4, 3/8, 2/4, 3/8, 2/4, 3/8, 2/4, 3/8, 4/8, 3/8, 2/4, 5/8, 2/4, 3/4.

Version B (Corresponds to the first 2 verses of text)
4/8, 5/8, 4/8, 5/8, 4/8, 5/8, 4/8, 5/8, 3/4, →2/4, 3/8, 5/8, 3/4, 3/8, 2/4,
     3/8, 2/4, 3/8, 2/4, 3/8, 2/4, 3/8, 4/8, 3/8, 2/4, 5/8, 2/4, 3/4.

Verse 3 of the text would correspond to measures 51–67, where both Versions **A** and **B** come together. Grainger uses massive unison scoring with the harmonies (in G Minor) found in the saxophone, trumpet, and trombone parts. Additionally, Grainger specifies that the trumpets triple-tongue as fast as possible with no set number of notes to the beat. A fourth verse would be represented by the music found in measures 68–84. The melody is now found in the saxophones and horns with a fresh new set of harmonies. Both verses 3 and 4 are identical in length (17 measures) and fit the text perfectly.

The final verse, represented in measures 85–103 is the same length (19 measures) as the opening verse, and is scored for a quartet of soloists including piccolo, oboe, bassoon, and E♭ clarinet. Set in the key of F Minor, it matches the key of Version **A**, but with an instrumentation that more closely resembles Version **B**. Leave it to Percy Grainger to craft an ending that would be suitable for either Version **A** or **B** for performance!

The fourth movement, titled *The Brisk Young Sailor* (who returned to wed his True Love), is eloquently captured on recording of 3 August 1906 by Mrs. Thompson, originally from Liverpool, but living in Barrow-on-Humber, North Lincolnshire. Mrs. Thompson's recording sounds as if she is in the key of G Major. The microfilm collection at the Library of Congress included a manuscript score for piano in C Major dated 7 June 1936 (based on sketches from about 1920 and reproduced on the following page). It includes the text of the folk song in the lower portion of the page as well as credit to Mrs. Thompson in the lower right hand corner.

Grainger noted two verses of this folk song in C Major, adjusting the key to B♭ Major for the wind band, expanding this movement to a theme and four variations of the original tune. It is interesting that the 1937 wind band score follows the 1936 piano score, not only in melodic and rhythmic detail, but in most of the articulation marks as well. Fredrick Fennell's 1987 full score edition is also well marked for both dynamics and articulations; two expressive elements central to an acceptable interpretation of this piece.

The War Song, *Lord Melbourne*, sung by Mr. George Wray at Brigg, Lincolnshire on 28 July 1906 is a variant of *The Duke of Marlborough*, a Sussex folk song. Although the melodic line from *The Duke of Marlborough* is varied in the *Lord Melbourne* setting, both contain approximately 35 notes, identical to the number Grainger used in the opening fanfare of the wind band score. The absence of key signature, free time, and varied tempi all characterize Grainger's approach to capturing the essence of this tune. While the following example only shows the first verse, Grainger's version printed in Volume III of the *Journal of the Folk-Song Society* includes all five verses in a through-composed version, thus capturing all of the melodic as well as rhythmic nuances of the folksinger, George Wray.[17]

Thrice phonographed and noted by Percy Grainger.   SUNG BY MR. GEORGE WRAY,
Phonograph record A   AT BRIGG, LINCOLNSHIRE, JULY 28TH, 1906.
Sung in (A-flat ? A Nautral)

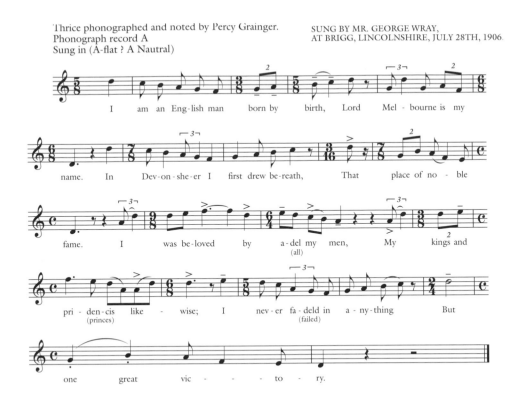

In Frederick Fennell's third article on *Lincolnshire Posy* (*The Instrumentalist*, 1980), he recalled a visit he had with Percy Grainger in early January 1958, during which they talked about the conductor's role in making *Lord Melbourne* work. Grainger's reply was that the answer was in the words.[18] Volume III of the *Journal of the Folk Song Society* provides the following text:

> I am an Englishman born by birth,
> Lord Melbourne is my name.
> In Devonshire I first drew breath,
> That place of noble fame.[19]

Grainger reminded Fennell of the drunkard at the local pub in Brigg, where the regulars boasted of a man who was the best singer of "the Lord", as he called it. The first word of each line was stretched by the singer, almost as if the man were trying to remember the next word before plunging into his performance.[20]

> I am a N-o-ble E-ng-lish-man,
> Lord Mel-bourne i-s my-name.
> I ne-ver l-o-st an-y bat-tle,
> but won great v-ic-tory.

This second text matches exactly the way Grainger scored the opening fanfare in the fifth movement. Two highly rhythmic variations follow, both containing frequent changes of meter. These variations are separated by a wonderful harmonic moment where the full ensemble sonority of the D Major triad releases into a D minor 9th chord, played at pianississimo (*ppp*). Grainger crafts the next variation to give the listener the impression of whistling as the solo piccolo (doubled two octaves lower by oboe) presents the *Lord Melbourne* tune. The grand fanfare that marked the beginning of the movement returns again to solidify the ending as well as present a neat bookends approach to framing the movement.

The sixth and concluding movement is titled *The Lost Lady Found* (Dance Song). It was originally made known to Grainger by Lucy E. Broadwood (to whom the setting is dedicated), from the singing of her Lincolnshire nurse, Mrs. Hill from Stamford in 1893 and later published in *The Journal of The Folk Song Society*.[21]

An examination of the nine stanzas of text helps to paint a clear picture of the story behind the music. A look at the original setting of the folk song reveals a strophic setting in D Dorian for these nine verses. In another version collected by Lucy E. Broadwood found in *English Traditional Songs and Carols*, we see the same strophic setting for all nine verses with an alternation of harmonic material between verses 1, 3, 5, 7, 9 and verses 2, 4, 6, 8.[21] It should be noted here certain variants of *The Lost Lady Found*, are sung to the tune of *Green Bushes*. However, the version of *Green Bushes* used by Vaughan Williams in his **English Folk Song Suite** is different than the version of used by Grainger in **Lincolnshire Posy**.

A triumph of orchestration occurs in Grainger's masterful setting of these nine verses in the wind band score. Verse 1 is scored in unison with written directions by Grainger (*short*) to match the text. Verse 2 (measures 17–33), features staccato brass punctuation on downbeats which adds interest to this musical story. Verse 3 (measures 33–49), features a syncopated horn part, referred to by some conductors as "Lame Duck Viennese".[22] A quartet of woodwind instruments accompanying the piccolo solo characterize the music of Verse 4 (measures 49–65), for which Grainger asks for *gently, feelingly*. One can ascertain why by simply examining the text. Additional instruments enter in Verse 5 (measures 65–81), as the story continues. The horns are marked *"to the fore"* in Verse 6 (measures 81–97), as the Lost Lady flies into her lover's arms. In Verse 7 (measures 97–113), and Verse 8 (measures 113–129), the syncopated horn part returns as the story builds to the climax in Verse 9 (measures 130-end). The text for Verse 9 reads as follows:

> Then straight from the gallows they lead him away,
> The **bells they did ring,** and the music did play;
> Every house in the valley with mirth did resound,
> As soon as they heard the lost lady was found.

Grainger summons a variety of what he calls "tuneful percussion" instruments, including Xylophone, Glockenspiel, Tubular Chimes, and Handbells in octaves to play during the final verse, in keeping with the exact words of the text. In the absence of Handbells, conductors could employ the use of Crotales as well as Parsifal Bells in this section. In John Bird's Biography of Percy Grainger, the following thoughts were expressed by Grainger in regard to tuneful percussion:

> And what are we to think of the lack of vision, lack of innate musicality, shown by 'high-brow' composers and conductors in their neglect of the exquisite 'tuneful percussion' instruments invented and perfected in America and else-where during the last 30 or 40 years—metal and wooden marimbas, staff bells, vibraphones, nabimbas, dulcitone, etc.? Yet these same 'classicists'—who prob-ably consider these mellow and delicate-toned instruments too 'low brow' to be admitted into the holy precincts of the symphony orchestra—endure with-out protest the everlasting thumping of the kettle-drums (which with brutal monotony wipes out all chord-clearness) in the Haydn-Mozart-Beethoven orchestrations! The truth is that most 'high brows' are much more 'low brow' than they themselves suspect!
>
> In this connection it is interesting to note that it is only the most harsh-toned tuneful-percussion instruments (glockenspiel, xylophone, tubular chimes) that have found a place in the symphony orchestra thus far. Can it be that the sym-phony orchestra prizes stridence of tone *only* in such instruments? If not, why has no place been found for the mellow-toned metal marimba (the continua-tion downwards of the glockenspiel) and the gentle-toned wooden marimba (the continuation downwards of the xylophone)? Perhaps because their quality of tone is too refined to be heard amidst the harsh sound-jumble of the sym-phony orchestra? If so, it is high time we revised our symphony orchestrations in the direction of a delicacy and refinement that can accommodate the subtler creations of modern instrument-building geniuses such as Deagan and others.
>
> To use, orchestrally, a glockenspiel without a metal marimba, a xylophone without a wooden marimba, is just as absurd and incomplete as it would be to use piccolo without flute, violins without lower strings, the two top octaves of the piano without the lower octaves. Let us get rid of this barbarism as soon as we can![23]

A four-page sketch score, located in the Library of Congress and dated 10 August 1910 shows Grainger already working on a version of *The Lost Lady Found* for Wom-en's and Men's Chorus with Brass accompaniment. This Lincolnshire dialect song was set in late 1910 and has been recorded by the Monteverdi Choir and the English

Country Gardiner Orchestra under the direction of John Eliot Gardiner in 1996. (John Eliot Gardiner is the great-nephew of H. Balfour Gardiner, organizer and financier of the series of concerts of British Music given by Percy Grainger in 1912 and 1913.)[24]

Lincolnshire Posy is a great wind band masterwork that invites much more in-depth study than this text provides. Grainger's painstaking efforts to collect, record, notate, orchestrate and arrange hundreds of folk songs during his lifetime as well as his continued efforts over a quarter of a century to work with these tunes resulting in his six-movement Suite are most impressive. Equally impressive are the efforts over the years by a host of dedicated conductors, spearheaded by Frederick Fennell, to finally produce the full score to *Lincolnshire Posy* that Percy Grainger unfortunately did not write for his wind band masterpiece.[25]

ENDNOTES

1. David Tall, *The Percy Grainger Companion* (London: Thames Publishing, 1981), 55.

2. John Bird, 2nd Rev. ed., *Percy Grainger* (London: Oxford University Press, 1999), 189.

3. David S. Josephson, review of *The Wind Music of Percy Aldridge Grainger*, by Thomas C. Slattery, *Current Musicology* 16 (1973): 79.

4. Mark Grauer, "Grainger's Lost Letters on Lincolnshire Posy," *The Instrumentalist* 47/1 (1992): 12–17.

5. Mark Grauer, "Grainger's Lost Letters on Lincolnshire Posy," *The Instrumentalist* 47/1 (1992): 15.

6. Percy Aldridge Grainger, Program Notes to *Lincolnshire Posy* (New York and London: G. Schirmer, 1940. Reprint Milwaukee, WI: Hal Leonard Publishing Corporation), iv.

7. Cecil J. Sharp, *Journal of The Folk Song Society*, vol. II (London: Baricott and Pearce, 1905–1906), 22.

8. Barry Peter Ould, Liner Notes to Percy Grainger: Orchestral Works, *Chandos CD9493* (1996): 7.

9. Richard Hickox, Percy Grainger: Orchestral Works, *Chandos CD9493* (1996).

10. Cecil J Sharp, *Journal of The Folk Song Society*, vol. II (London: Baricott and Pearce, 1905–1906), 22.

11. Helen Reeves, Melbourne, Australia to Dorothy Sara Lee, Library of Congress, 30 November 1981, Grainger Folder, Folklife Reading Room, Library of Congress, Washington, DC.

12. Frederick Fennell, "Basic Band Repertory—Lincolnshire Posy," *The Instrumentalist* 34/10 (1980): 45.

13. Bob Thompson, Liner Notes to *Unto Brigg Fair*, Leader LP 4050 (1908).

14. Ibid.

15. Percy Aldridge Grainger, *Journal of The Folk Song Society*, vol. III (London: Baricott and Pearce, 1908–1909), 186.

16. Richard Miles, ed., *Teaching Music Through Performance in Band* (Chicago: GIA Publications, Inc., 1997), 412.

17. Percy Aldridge Grainger, *Journal of The Folk Song Society*, vol. III (London: Baricott and Pearce, 1908–1909), 200–206.

18. Frederick Fennell, "Basic Band Repertory—Lincolnshire Posy Part III," *The Instrumentalist* 35/3 (1980): 30.

19. Percy Aldridge Grainger, *Journal of The Folk Song Society*, vol. III (London: Baricott and Pearce, 1908–1909), 200–206.

20. Frederick Fennell, "Basic Band Repertory—Lincolnshire Posy Part III," *The Instrumentalist* 35/3 (1980): 30.

21. Lucy E. Broadwood, *English Traditional Songs and Carols* (Boosey & Co., 1908), 86–90.

22. Craig Kirchhoff, Lectures on Grainger's *Lincolnshire Posy*, Summer 1990, The University of Calgary, Alberta, Canada.

23. John Bird, *Percy Grainger* (London: Paul Elek, 1976), 288.

24. James Chater, Liner Notes from *Danny Boy*, Philips CD 446 657–2 (1996): 22.

25. Frederick Fennell, ed., Foreward to Full Score Edition, *Lincolnshire Posy* (Cleveland, Ohio: Ludwig Music Publishing Co., 1987), 2.

Molly on the Shore

Collected:	1907, Original setting for String 'four-some' or String Orchestra
Composed:	1907–1920, Copyright 1921 by Percy Grainger Published by Carl Fischer, Inc., New York
First Performance:	String Quartet version, December 1909 at the home of the von Glehns in Cheyne Walk 28 October 1910, Copenhagen by a ladies' amateur orchestra
Reprinted Edition:	1962, Copyright by Ella Viola Strom Grainger
New Critical Edition:	Published by Carl Fischer, Inc., New York, 2002

Percy Grainger had some rather characteristic comments about his early compositions, including *Molly on the Shore*. "One reason why things of mine like 'Molly' & 'Shepherd's Hey' are good is because there is so little gaiety & fun in them. Where other composers would have been jolly in setting such dance tunes I have been sad or furious. My dance settings are energetic rather than gay. They are more like Russian music than English music. They are sad like parts of Balakirev's 'Tamara' & fierce like the 'Trepak' in Tchaikovsky's 'Nutcracker'."[1]

Molly on the Shore is a work that served Grainger well during the years when he traveled as both a concert pianist and guest conductor. Some notable performances during which *Molly on the Shore* was programmed include:

* 12 May, 1912 at the Aeolian Hall, London
* 19 October, 1912 at Queen's Hall, England
* April 1914 at Torquay
* 23 January, 1915 by Walter Damrosch and the Symphony Society of New York
* 18 June, 1920 for a Goldman Band concert on the green at Columbia University

Molly on the Shore is composed in a strophic form similar to works such as *Country Gardens, Shepherd's Hey* and even several movements of *Lincolnshire Posy*. While Grainger never invested the time to produce full scores for any of his wind band works, he always referred to his condensed scores as 'compressed' full scores and included more information about the instrumentation than one would expect to find in a condensed score. "When working at a composition for instruments or voices, moreover, he would adopt an intriguing procedure which was a reversal of the normal practice. It was not uncommon for him to spread virgin sheets of manuscript paper around the room on tables, side-boards, chairs, and music stands set up for the purpose and begin by writing out the instrumental and vocal parts. Upon completion of this stage of the task, he would then distil a full score or one of his 'compressed' full scores from the parts."[2] Composers including Nicolai Rimsky-Korsakov and Robert Russell Bennett were said to have worked in this same fashion.

Grainger was also a prolific annotator, and his compressed scores contain a wealth of useful information to assist the conductor in understanding the background of his compositions. Information provided by Grainger on the title page of *Molly on the Shore* indicates that the piece is based on two Cork Reel tunes taken from the *Complete Petrie Collection of Ancient Irish Music* edited by Charles Villiers Stanford and published by Boosey & Co., London. These tunes include "Temple Hill" and "Molly on the Shore" and are listed as numbers 901 and 902 respectively in the collection. Grainger goes on to state that the dance tunes in their original form are printed on page 2 of the publication of *Molly on the Shore* for piano solo.[3] The publication of the complete collection of Dr. George Petrie's manuscripts of Irish Music in three volumes was accomplished by Sir Charles Villiers Stanford during the period of 1902–1905. Charles V. Stanford (1852–1924) was born and raised in Dublin, attended Cambridge University, and went on to compose in every musical form. He served as professor of composition at the Royal College of Music from 1883–1923 and listed among his notable students the names of Gustav Holst and Ralph Vaughan Williams. Stanford took an interest in Grainger in 1904 and was one of two famous conductors (the other being Hans Richter) who took an interest in helping Grainger establish himself as a concerto soloist. Grainger became devoted to Stanford and within three years had selected two tunes from the Complete Petrie Collection for his use with *Molly on the Shore*.

As we have already seen with *Lincolnshire* Posy, Grainger used all of the thematic material from the "Molly on the Shore" and "Temple Hill" as source material for *Molly on the Shore*, and added four original short melodic motives to serve as counter melodic material. The only adjustment made by Grainger from the original Cork Reel settings was to transpose the key up one-half step from the original of G Major to the key of A-flat Major for wind band. The piece is given a tempo marking of *presto* with the speed of the half note equaling between 120 and 126. The final tempo for performance by a wind band, however, is subject to several considerations. These considerations have been succinctly described by R. Mark Rogers, Director of Publications, Southern Music Company, in his writing about the technical considerations in performing *Molly on the Shore*. "The musical demands of the band version are perhaps higher than that for any of the orchestral versions for the simple reason that the Cork Reel tunes which Grainger chose for his setting are "fiddle" pieces and, as such, are idiomatic for performance by string instruments, taking advantage of open strings, various characteristic bowing techniques, and a sort of "perpetual motion" playing that is relatively simple for strings but very difficult for wind instruments to achieve."[4] Given the fact that Percy Grainger originally set *Molly on the Shore* for string quartet, his tempo indication of 120–126 to the half-note makes sense for performance of these Cork Reel tunes by strings. However, brief survey of several recorded versions of Grainger's *Molly on the Shore* reveals the following tempo indications:

Version	Artist	Date	Timing	Tempo	Source
Piano	Percy Grainger	May 1920	3:17	132–134	Nimbus 8809
Violin & Piano	Sillito/Milne	May 1998	3:37	114–118	Chandos 9746

Wind Orchestra	London Wind Orchestra	1992	3:45	104–108	WHL2067
Wind Orchestra	Royal Northern College	December 1996	3:53	102–106	Chandos 9549
Orchestra	BBC Symphony	April 1997	4:06	96–98	Chandos 9584

The beauty of Grainger's wind band setting of *Molly on the Shore* has to do more with the craftsmanship of the work itself, and not simply a blind adherence to the tempo indication. With attention to proper style as well as clarity of articulation, wonderful performances of this piece can take place at tempos that are significantly slower than Grainger's original marking.

At the core of introduction is a one-measure ostinato that repeats itself fifteen times at the beginning of the work. In his article from the Basic Band Repertory series from the *Instrumentalist*, Frederick Fennell had this to say about the approach to the ostinatos that are such an important part of this piece.

> The *pizzicato* characteristic, as sound, may be described: perfectly articulate, desirably resonant. If obvious technical wind approaches do not produce the proper sound, the conductor should not hesitate to invite string players to bring their instruments to band rehearsal for what could be a vivid demonstration that might long transcend the movement or the piece. In any case the conductor should avoid a sound that is brittle and dry, but still secure proper spacing of the notes from all who contribute to the five *ostinatos* so vital to this music. In the original string version the opening ostinato I for instance, employed four highly resonant open strings G–D/D–A from the violin and cello, a resource not to be duplicated by wind instruments, to be sure, but a tonal character wind performers should strive to approximate.[5]

After a short, two-measure introduction in A-flat Major, the main theme of "Molly on the Shore" is presented in the 1st clarinet and alto clarinet over a low woodwind ostinato (measures 1–10).

The original Cork Reel, "Molly on the Shore" is actually comprised of three eight-measure phrases. The second part of the "Molly" theme is presented from measures 11–18 using the same scoring from the opening phrase.

Beginning in measure 19, the third part of the "Molly" theme is heard in bass clarinet and bassoons with an accompaniment provided by the clarinets.

The only change that Grainger makes from the original Cork Reel is a slight rhythmic alteration in measure 23 to maintain the eighth-note triplet feel throughout the phrase. The previous figure has been engraved using the rhythms found in the original setting from George Petrie's collection so that an immediate comparison can be made to the wind band score.

The main theme returns at measure 27 in 1st and 2nd clarinets and 1st alto saxophone, and the second part of the Molly theme is presented at measure 35 along with a punctuated accompaniment full band and percussion.

The theme based on "Temple Hill" first appears in measure 43 in the piccolo, flutes, clarinets; this theme is balanced by a slower moving original theme by Grainger scored above the "Temple Hill" theme played in the oboes, soprano and alto saxophones, cornets, and horns (measures 43–46).

Beginning in measure 51, the second part of the "Temple Hill" theme is now presented as its own free-standing melody in the upper woodwinds against punctuated quarter note accompaniment in the rest of the band. While the tempo marking at the beginning of the piece is *presto*, conductors will initially be rehearsing this piece at a slower tempo using a light staccato two-beat pattern. However, when the second part of the "Temple Hill" theme at measure 51 appears, a change in conducting style to a more energized four-beat pattern (twice as fast) will help to keep the performers on task and prevent the tempo from slowing down.

A return to the first part of the "Molly on the Shore" theme beginning in measure 59 will allow the conductor to settle back into the light staccato two-beat pattern as the alto saxophone and cornet are highlighted.

Grainger begins to flex his compositional muscle as we note the return of the second part of the "Molly" theme beginning in measure 67, this time cast in stretto between piccolo, flutes, clarinets and oboes, 4th clarinets, saxophones, and 2nd cornets. From measure 75–82, the third part of the "Molly" theme is heard; this time, however, Grainger has removed the three eighth-notes and substituted a dotted quarter in an effort to ease the tension of the piece and produce a more legato phrase. Of course, Grainger never used the word legato in his scores; in fact, all reference to Italian terminology was replaced with Grainger's own English equivalents. In this case, Grainger prints the phrase *very feelingly* at measure 75 to describe his musical intent. This effect can be enhanced by insisting that performers playing the accompaniment quartet notes observe their full value unless articulated otherwise. Some conductors request that the players add tenuto marks over the quarter note accompaniment figures in measures 75–77 and again in measures 79–80.

The snare drum makes an important entrance in measure 83 that continues with a passage that extends through measure 90. Unfortunately, this is not included in the 3-line compressed score, but should be copied out from the snare drum part and written into the score to ensure proper rhythmic alignment with the ensemble as the first part of the "Molly" theme is again heard in the clarinets. Measure 83 also introduces material that can be traced back to the previous eight-measure theme, although this time varied, and set in contrapuntal fashion against the return of the first part of the "Molly" theme. There is an interesting connection between this new countermelody (measures 83–86) as played by the oboes, 2nd clarinet, alto clarinet, alto and tenor saxophones, 4th cornet, and 3rd & 4th horns, and material heard in as the melodic line from measures 75–78. While Grainger's adaptation of the second part of the "Molly" theme (measures 11–14) maintains the descending direction of the line (see measures 75–78), his new adaptation (measures 83–86) begins precisely where the previous line ended, on concert A-flat, but now moves in an ascending direction.

Beginning in measure 91, the third part of the "Molly" theme can be heard in flutes, piccolo and clarinets (1st part has 8 measures rest), but is set against a fuller accompaniment. Measure 99 marks the return of the "Temple Hill" theme, first heard (measure 43) in the clarinets. This time, however, it is scored only in the 1st clarinet part and is written a major second lower against pedal tones on the pitches of A♭ and E♭. The return of the second part of the "Temple Hill" theme is heard in measure 107, and is also written a major second lower than its initial appearance (in measure 51). As the pedal tones continue through this phrase, it becomes evident that Grainger has shifted the tonality to the parallel minor key of A-flat.

A comparison of the scoring from measures 43–46 (refer to page 78) to measures 115–118 reveals a nearly identical approach, with the exception that the music is still a major second lower than before, allowing for the key of G-flat Major to be established through some well-placed courtesy accidentals, along with the addition of the vibraphone part (first introduced from measures 91–98).

Grainger continues to establish the new tonality of G-flat Major through the next phrase (measures 123–130) as the second part of the "Temple Hill" theme is presented in very similar scoring fashion to the earlier appearance (from measures 51–58), but written a major second lower similar to the return of the melody in measure 107. Suddenly, like rounding the corner to meet an old friend, we find ourselves right back in A-flat Major beginning in measure 131 with the return of the first part of the "Molly" theme written in identical pitch and rhythmic notation to the first statement from measures 3–10. The second part of the "Molly" theme follows (measures 139–146), this time harmonized similar to the first appearance (measures 35–42), but with some different voicings. The obvious difference to the listener will be the introduction of the long descending chromatic lines in measures 143–146 which fuel the virtuosic display. When the first part of the "Molly" theme is presented in measures 147–154, Grainger creates a brand new countermelody in the cornet and alto saxophone parts, which he marks *feelingly*. A whimper of the third part of the "Molly" theme is heard from measures 155–162 (courtesy of the 4th clarinets), but seems to give way in most performances to the rapid descending chromatic scale passages which generally overtake this section of the piece.

The final statement of the first "Temple Hill" theme occurs from measures 163–170 and is now written a minor third lower in comparison to the 1st clarinet part in measures 99–106. Since this earlier return of the first "Temple Hill" theme set against pedal tones of A♭ and E♭ suggested a tonality of A-flat minor, a connection can be made to Grainger's re-use of this material in measures 163–170, this time a minor third lower and set against pedal tones of F and C to provide a sense of the music now being in F minor. The final statement of the second "Temple Hill" theme follows, also written a minor third lower than the earlier return of this material (see measures 107–114). The first part of the "Molly" theme returns for a final appearance in measures 179–186 and is stated in identical pitches and rhythms of the original (measures 3–10). Grainger concludes the composition with a final statement of the second part of the "Molly" theme, this time harmonized by the flutes, passed to the clarinets with very little accompaniment and a gradual diminuendo (which Grainger referred to as *soften*) down to a marked dynamic of *pppp*, only to surprise the listener with a final A-flat Major chord marked with the dynamic of *ffff*.

In 1936 Grainger wrote: "In these youthful musical thots of mine there are tucked away some flashes that are soul-revealing—occasional chords, melodic lines, phrases that are truly Nordic, truly British, truly new-world, truly Australian."[6] In Percy Aldridge Grainger's *Molly on the Shore*, we are treated to moments of this soul-revealing quality that permeated his work.

ENDNOTES

1. John Bird, 3rd Rev. ed., *Percy Grainger* (London: Oxford University Press, 1999), 70–71.

2. John Bird, 3rd Rev. ed., *Percy Grainger* (London: Oxford University Press, 1999), 102.

3. Percy Aldridge Grainger, "Molly on the Shore," title page of conductor score, 1921, Carl Fischer, Inc., New York.

4. Richard Miles, ed., *Teaching Music through Performance in Band*, vol. 3, *Molly on the Shore*, by R. Mark Rogers (Chicago: GIA Publications, Inc., 2000), 390–391.

5. Frederick Fennell, "Molly on the Shore by Percy Aldridge Grainger," *The Instrumentalist* (1983): 24.

6. John Bird, 3rd Rev. ed., *Percy Grainger* (London: Oxford University Press, 1999), 71.

English Waltz from the Youthful Suite for Orchestra

Composed: Scored between 1899–1901, revised 1940–1947
                  Published in 1945 by Schott for Orchestra with Piano
                  Published in 1947 by Schott/Schirmer for Two Pianos (4 hands)
                  Transcribed for Band in 1987 by David McKinney
                  Band version published in 1999 by Southern Music Company
Performance: 29 April, 1960 Grainger gave his last public performance at
                  Dartmouth College in Hanover, New Hampshire which included
                  A two piano performance of *English Waltz*

The final study in this text includes an early work by Percy Grainger which was almost lost to the wind band world, had it not been for the formidable efforts from Grainger devotee David McKinney, and subsequent support from R. Mark Rogers of Southern Music Company. David McKinney's scholarly work from 1985–1987 while a graduate student at the University of Arkansas allowed him to produce a full score wind band setting of *English Waltz* working from the "compressed" full score that Grainger had created for the fifth movement of the *Youthful Suite for Orchestra*. McKinney contacted Stewart Manville, Grainger Archivist of the Percy Grainger Library in White Plains, New York to secure permission to proceed with the transcription project.

David McKinney explained the journey to the source as follows. "Next, I had to get the score. Every phone call I made led me somewhere else: I was stunned to discover that **not one** of the larger orchestral libraries or publishers in the USA at that time (1985–1986) had a copy of Grainger's *Youthful Suite* for orchestra—including Ebble Orchestra House in Iowa, and Carl Fischer in New York, who published a lot of Grainger. I made calls to every conceivable orchestral publisher, coast to coast, through the US. But through Carl Fischer, I was put onto calling Schott Publishing Co., Ltd in London, England—which I did—and they engraved a copy for me, for the price of 18 pounds."[1]

Southern Music Company editor Mark Rogers subjected the parts from David McKinney's project to the same procedures that Grainger used in pieces such as *Colonial Song, Country Gardens, Irish Tune from County Derry, Molly on the Shore, Shepherd's Hey, and The 'Gumsuckers' March* in order to ensure that the spirit of *English Waltz* had been retained. As a result, the world of wind band has acquired a recent "chosen gem" as a result of the creativity of Percy Grainger. The transcription of Grainger's *English Waltz*, Movement 5 from the *Youthful Suite* for Orchestra, was premiered as part of a full Grainger concert in April 1987 by the University of Arkansas Symphonic Band, Eldon A. Janzen, Director of Bands, conducting. A score and recording were subsequently sent to Stewart Manville, and on 15 June 1987 David McKinney received the following letter.

"Dear Mr. McKinney,

You are correct in assuming that I would be pleased with your band transcription of Grainger's *English Waltz.*

On occasion it seems a bit bottom-heavy with tuba, and you may wish to consider lightening those moments before committing it for publication.

Here, gladly, is permission for you to make band transcriptions of the remaining movements of *Youthful Suite*.

> With every good wish.
> Sincerely,
> Stewart R. Manville"[2]

The *Youthful Suite* for Orchestra was created between the years of 1899–1901; it was then laid aside until the period of 1940–1947 when Grainger completed the project for performance. He also prepared a version for piano as well as piano four-hands between the years of 1943–1945. Just as we can unlock new ideas about the interpretation of those wind band pieces influenced by song through tracing the music back to its original root form, we can benefit from hearing performances of works for wind band that have been arranged in other versions. Examples for the *English Waltz* would be the versions performed by orchestra (see CHANDOS 9584) as well as piano (see CHANDOS 9895).

Richard Hickox is considered to be one of Britain's leading conductors, and has conducted the BBC Philharmonic, the City of London Sinfonia, and the Danish National Radio Symphony Orchestra in a total of seven recordings in Chandos' Grainger Edition. His recording of the fifth movement from the *Youthful Suite* allows an opportunity to hear the *English Waltz* performed by orchestra in a version which is identical in both form and design to the wind band version. While Grainger marks the waltz-speed as a dotted quarter note equaling 69, Hickox employs just a slightly faster tempo of dotted quarter equaling 72. Hickox also pulls back the tempo in the middle of the repeat of the third theme (measures 161–162) to allow the rising chromatic harmonies to settle before completing the thematic idea. This stretch allows the listener to hear the harmonic differences as this theme is repeated. With a performance time of 4:23 we are provided with an excellent interpretation of how the wind band version might be performed.

Penelope Thwaites graduated with a First Class Honours degree in music from Melbourne University, Australia and is a leading authority on the music of Grainger. As a pianist and concerto soloist she has appeared with leading orchestras in England, the Unites States, and Australia and has completed six recordings in Chandos' Grainger Edition. Her performance of Grainger's *English Waltz* allows the listener to really focus on Grainger's beautiful use of melodic line as well as the rich harmonic language found in this work. Since the phrase endings that provide the transitions in this piece can be problematic for wind band musicians, a careful listening to the solo piano version as recorded by Penelope Twaites will help students to hear the subtle changes of harmony that make these transitions actually sound quite seamless if performed correctly. With a recorded performance time of 5:23 we have an opportunity to hear this music unfold in a most lyrical manner. The piano version of *English Waltz* is also an identical match to the wind band version in both form and design, but does include moments of virtuosic display as one would come to expect from a pianist/composer of Grainger's caliber. Interestingly, Grainger achieves this level of virtuosity without sacrificing any of the melodic ideas found in the orchestral or wind band versions.

An important consideration for an effective performance of *English Waltz* is attention to the required instrumentation. One immediately notices the instrumentation list includes soprano saxophone, double bass, harp (one or more), piano (one or more), and tuneful percussion (six or more players) in order to complete the wind band sonority. These are not options; the parts for harp, piano, and a minimum of six mallet-keyboard percussionists are required to achieve the balances required in this score. Instrumental conductors who are faced with the challenge of keeping so many percussionists busy during concert band season as a result of having a large marching percussion section in the Fall season should welcome Grainger's *English Waltz* as one of those pieces that can accommodate as many percussionists as are available. I have achieved great success in programming *English Waltz* as part of an honor band festival by supplementing the tuneful percussion requirements with students drawn from the host director's institution. (I have also employed this technique with the *Lost Lady Found* from Grainger's *Lincolnshire Posy* as a way of meeting the spirit of Grainger's request for the use of tuneful percussion.)

English Waltz is based on three original themes composed and scored by Percy Grainger when he was between the age of 17–20. Although born in Melbourne, mother and son moved to Frankfurt in 1895, and by age thirteen, Percy was enrolled in the Hoch Conservatorium, an institution that was considered to be among the finest in Europe. Rose and Percy also had the opportunity to travel to France, England, and Scotland during the spring and summer months of 1900. Of the trip to Glasgow, Grainger fondly remembered his three-day hike through the mountains and lochs in the area of West Argyllshire. "He later described this as the most important single artistic influence in his life. His two *Hill-Songs*, which can be numbered amongst his finest compositions, were commenced within a year of his return to Frankfurt, and bagpipe-like sororities are easily discernable in these works."[3]

English Waltz opens with the oboes presenting an introductory four-measure motive which closes as a fermata on the dominant seventh of B-flat Major. This motive is heard several more times throughout the work, used each time as a short transition to repeat the primary theme. The primary theme (Theme A) is presented in the 1st alto saxophone, bassoons, and horns from measures 5–20 using the four measures from the introduction (measure 21–24) as a means of ending the phrase to creating a turn-around for repeat (the sound of a first ending with writing a first ending).

Theme A is repeated in measures 25–44, this time scored in upper woodwinds and soprano saxophone. This time the phrase ending is different; Grainger employs sixteenth-note triplets to create a sweeping finish that calls for dexterity of fingering in woodwinds, doubled by 1st trumpet.

For the second theme (Theme B), Grainger shifts the tonal center to D-flat Major; this theme is heard in the saxophones from measures 45–62, and repeated in the upper woodwinds from measures 63–78.

A phrase extension is used (in measures 61–62) to create a slight difference in the presentation of the same thematic material, heard back-to-back. An eight-measure bridge section (with key signature changed back to B-flat Major) based on the opening introductory motive leads to a return of Theme A (measures 87–106), this time stated in 1st trumpet and 1st trombone (cued in 2nd trombone). Percy Grainger's marking *to the fore* gives a clear indication that these instruments are to play as soloists. The sweeping finish used in the initial repeat of the Theme A (measures 41–44) is heard again (measures 103–106), this time scored in all of the clarinet parts (including alto clarinet) but omitted in the saxophone parts.

The third theme (Theme C) makes its first appearance beginning in measure 107 in the flute, clarinet, soprano and tenor sax parts as the key signature changes to E-flat Major.

Within the thirty-two measures we observe some interesting rhythms, most notably the accompaniment in the trumpet and trombone parts from measures 119–123.

Performers must count very carefully (after having practiced these measures diligently with a metronome) to ensure that the rhythm in these five measures is not cheated in any way. On the heels of that phrase ending comes the next rhythmic challenge (measures 124–126), that of correctly aligning the rhythm of the "oom-pah" figures in low winds, 3rd trombone, tuba, double bass, and timpani against those of the trumpets, horns, trombones, and snare drum. Again, some persistent individual practice with a metronome will go a long way to cleaning up what could be a potential ensemble nightmare as the lyrical C Theme glides above the accompaniment. The repeat of the C Theme takes place from measures 139–170, this time featuring the 1st and 2nd trumpets, 1st and 2nd trombones, and euphonium as a new countermelody is introduced in the piccolo, flute, oboe, English horn, bassoons, alto saxophone, (muted) 3rd trumpet, and horns.

The B Theme makes its return from measures 171–208, but this time in the key of G-flat. It does keep to the same design as its first appearance (measures 45–62), that of two eight-measure phrases in which the first (see measures 61–62) has a two measure phrase extension (this time in measures 187–188).

However, Grainger finishes the final presentation of the B Theme with a four-measure phrase extension (measures 205–208), which features the 1st and 2nd horns. An eight-measure bridge section based on the introduction follows (measure 209–216), with a return to the key signature of B-flat Major. This sets up a sparkling return of the A Theme (measures 217–236) which features a soli between piccolo and bassoon with light accompaniment figures in clarinets, supported by harp and piano. A sweeping crescendo with sixteenth-note triplet figures in the woodwinds (clarinets have accompaniment) leads into the final presentation of the A Theme from measures 237–256, this time scored for full band with alto and tenor saxophone, trumpets, 1st and 2nd trombones, and euphoniums (all marked *to the fore*) carrying the melody. The same style of "Lame Duck Viennese" accompaniment as used in the final movement of *Lincolnshire Posy* appears as the primary accompaniment figure in these two phrases, which finishes with the sweeping sixteenth-note triplet figures (measures 253–256) in the woodwinds, scored almost identically to the first appearance in measures 41–44.

The final presentation of the C Theme (measures 257–280) does not disappoint; this is the very moment that Grainger has saved for the entrance of the tuneful percussion instruments, which include bells, xylophone (Grainger called it Hammerwood), marimba, vibraphone (Grainger called it Wooden and Metal Marimbas), tubular chimes and Swiss Handbells (crotales are a nice substitute) all played in octaves, if possible. The musical material for the tuneful percussion is a reappearance of the countermelody used beginning in measure 140.

A heavy three-measure transition from measures 281–283 sets up the Coda section from measures 284–299. It is interesting to note that Grainger inserts two measures of music in 2/4 meter (measures 292–293) amidst a piece that is written in 3/8 meter, but felt in "one." Students performing the work simply need to be reminded that Grainger wanted the eighth note to equal the eighth note, so the effect is simply one of moving from 3/8 to 4/8 and back again to 3/8. The 2/4 meter signature was simply a notational convenience for flutes, oboes, English horn, 1st clarinets, bassoons, and trumpets. The piece ends in glorious fashion (measure 294–299), with a sustained B♭ Major chord in high winds, trumpets, and horns; a descending scale passage in the lower voices (played as double-sticking sixteenth notes in mallet keyboards), and with a flourish of sixteenth-note triplet B♭ arpeggios in clarinets and saxophones to bring the piece to a close on a *fff* B♭ Major chord. Conductors may wish to allow the tuneful percussion parts to ring after the release of the final chord by the winds.

In closing this chapter on Percy Grainger, I wish to acknowledge the efforts of Eugene Corporon who, in February 2001, brought Grainger biographer John Bird from England to Denton, Texas to address those of us in attendance at the College Band Directors National Association Conference. The third edition of his Grainger biography had just been issued, and many of us were eager to obtain a revised copy to benefit from Bird's continuing research on Percy Grainger. The earlier editions of 1976 and 1982 have long been staples in the research of those engaged in the study of Grainger, and the 1999 edition promised to include new biographical material. It is an interesting coincidence that in the very same month, the Instrumentalist magazine published an insightful article by James Croft entitled *John Bird's Fascinating Quest To Understand Percy Grainger*. When asked about an appraisal of Grainger's melodic gifts, John Bird replied, "I am anxious to speak up for Grainger as a melodist. Just listen to the superb melodies in the Kipling settings for choir or voices and instruments with melodies that can break your heart. *The Gum-suckers March* and *Over the Hills and Far Away* aren't such bad tunes, are they? How about *Colonial Song, English Waltz*, and the two *Hill Songs*? The climatic melody in *The Warriors* could match anything Elgar wrote for its goose-pimple factor. I disagree with the critics here: I think where original melody was concerned, Grainger was a man on top of his game."[4]

Percy Grainger presented his last public performance on April 29, 1960 as part of the Third Annual Festival of Music at Dartmouth College. His lecture was entitled "The Influence of Folk-song on Art Music" and he illustrated his lecture with two-piano versions of five of his compositions, including *English Waltz*. How fitting that one of the last compositions Grainger performed would become the newest addition to the wind band repertoire.

ENDNOTES

1. David McKinney, Director of Bands, The University of Western Ontario, interview by author, 2 June 2004, Burlington, Ontario (via e-mail).

2. David McKinney, Director of Bands, The University of Western Ontario, interview by author, 2 June 2004, Burlington, Ontario (via e-mail).

3. John Bird, 3rd Rev. ed., *Percy Grainger* (London: Oxford University Press, 1999), 46.

4. James Croft, "John Bird's Fascinating Quest to Understand Percy Grainger." *The Instrumentalist* 55/7 (2001): 21.

A PERCY GRAINGER DISCOGRAPHY

Without doubt, some of the most exciting research on Percy Grainger is in the form of a current recording project initiated by **Chandos Records** in 1996. *The Grainger Edition*, Chandos's major new recording project, is a most ambitious undertaking—to record the complete music of Percy Grainger on twenty-five CDs. The series features Grainger's orchestral, chamber, solo song, choral and wind band music. Amongst Grainger's many folk-song arrangements are some of the world's best-known pieces, but the series also reveals a richly rewarding body of original and previously unrecorded work. The liner notes, researched and compiled by Barry Peter Ould, provide a single source of superb scholarship on Grainger, and the recorded performances have been equally well researched. Much reference has been made to Percy Grainger's ability to "dish it up" or create several versions of the same tune in different settings. This series of recordings provides living proof of those claims.

Volume 1, *Orchestral Works* (Chan 9493), features Richard Hickox conducting the BBC Philharmonic in twelve of Grainger's compositions. The tracks are as follows:

1.	'The Duke of Marlborough' Fanfare	2:27
2.	Colonial Song	5:23
3.	English Dance	8:56

4.	Shepherd's Hey	1:59
5.	There Were Three Friends	1:54
6.	Fisher's Boarding-House	6:36
7.	We Were Dreamers	3:49
8.	Harvest Hymn	3:16
9.	Blithe Bells	4:08
10.	Walking Tune	3:55
	Suite: 'In a Nutshell'	(20:20)
11.	I Arrival Platform Humlet	2:36
12.	II Gay but Wistful	3:15
13.	III Pastoral	10:16
14.	IV The 'Gum-suckers' March	8:27
15.	Green Bushes	8:27

Volume 2, *Songs for Baritone* (Chan 9503) is a collection including thirteen premiere recordings for baritone, featuring Stephen Varcoe and pianist Penelope Thwaites. Penelope Thwaites is a leading authority on Percy Grainger and was awarded the International Percy Grainger Society's Medallion in 1991 in recognition of her work. The tracks are as follows:

1.	Willow Willow	3:55
2.	Six Dukes Went Afishin'	2:19
3.	British Waterside	1:41
4.	The Pretty Maid Milkin' her Cow	1:22
5.	The Lost Lady Found (see *Lincolnshire Posy*)	2:44
6.	Creepin' Jane	4:08
7.	Bold William Taylor	3:39
8.–11.	Four settings from *Songs of the North*	8:38
12–17.	Six settings of Rudyard Kipling (1865–1936)	16:34
18.	Hard Hearted Barb'ra (H)Ellen	6:45
	Henry Wadsworth Longfellow (1807–1882)	
19.	The Secret of the Sea	3:30
	Arthur Conan Doyle (1859–1930)	
20.	Sailor's Chanty	3:06
21.	Shallow Brown	5:08

Penelope Thwaites and Stephen Varcoe appear again in **Volume 3,** *Works for Chorus and Orchestra* (Chan 9499), along with Mark Padmore, tenor; and Richard Hickox conducting the City of London Sinfonia and the Joyful Company Singers in a mixture of well-known and not so well-known pieces. The tracks are as follows:

1.	Shallow Brown	5:08
2.	Marching Tune	4:11
3.	I'm Seventeen Come Sunday (see *English Folk Song Suite*)	2:56
4.–5.	Two Sea Chanties	3:07
6.	Molly on the Shore	4:00

7.	Brigg Fair	3:09
8.	Early One Morning	2:55
9.	After-word	3:51
10.	There Was a Pig Went Out to Dig	1:57
11.	The Lonely Desert—Man Sees the Tents of the Happy Tides	2:32
	Oliver Wendell Holmes (1809–1894)	
12.	Thou Gracious Power	2:52
13.	County Derry Air	7:07
14.	Handel in the Strand	4:08
15.	Six Dukes Went Afishin'	4:00
	Rudyard Kipling (1865–1930)	
16.	Anchor Song	3:34
17.	Ye Banks and Braes O' Bonnie Doon	2:55

Volume 4, *Works for Wind Orchestra* (Chan 9549), features Timothy Reynish and Clark Rundell conducting the Royal Northern College of Music Wind Orchestra in twelve selections including:

1.	Hill Song No. 2	5:01
2.	Ye Banks and Braes O' Bonnie Doon	2:56
3.	Faeroe Island Dance	2:33
4.	The Lads of Wamphray March	7:52
5.	Irish Tune from County Derry	4:12
6.	Shepherd's Hey	2:02
7.	The Merry King	4:03
8.	Molly on the Shore	3:53
9.	Country Gardens	1:53
10.	Colonial Song	6:06
11.	The 'Gum-Suckers' March	3:46
	Lincolnshire Posy	15:40
12. 1	Dublin Bay (Lisbon)	1:27
13. 2	Harkstow Grange	2:57
14. 3	Rufford Park Poachers	3:47
15. 4	The Brisk Young Sailor	1:41
16. 5	Lord Melbourne	3:16
17. 6	The Lost Lady Found	2:19

Volume 5, *Works for Chorus and Orchestra 2* (Chan 9554), again features Richard Hickox, the City of London Sinfonia and the Joyful Company of Singers. Soloists include: Pamela Helen Stephen, mezzo-soprano; Mark Padmore, tenor; Stephen Varcone, baritone; Geoffrey Tozer, piano. Included in the eighteen tracks are seven premiere recordings, identified with an *.

1.	The Widow's Party*	3:59
2.	The Sea-Wife*	4:58
3.	The Running of Shindand	1:39

4.	We Have Fed Our Sea for a Thousand Years*	3:14
5.	Tiger-Tiger*	1:20
6.	The Love Song of Har Dyal*	2:54
7.	Country Gardens	2:20
8.	The Immovable Do	4:58
9.	Mock Morris	3:14
10.	Colleen Dhas	3:31
11.	Scotch Strathspey and Reel	7:08
12.	Dreamery*	2:24
13.	Colonial Song	5:31
14.	My Robin is to the Greenwood Gone	4:53
15.	Harvest Hymn	3:07
16.	Handel in the Strand	3:43
17.	Lord Maxwell's Goodnight*	3:18
18.	The Lost Lady Found (see *Lincolnshire Posy*)	2:53

Volume 6, *Orchestral Works 2* (Chan 9584), features the BBC Philharmonic under the baton of Richard Hickox. The tracks include:

1.–5.	Youthful Suite (see *English Waltz*)	25:36
6.	Molly On The Shore	4:06
7.	Irish Tune from County Derry	3:41
8.	Shepherd's Hey	1:56
9.	Country Gardens	2:17
10.	Early One Morning	3:32
11.	Handel in the Strand	3:59
12.	Mock Morris	3:19
13.	Dreamery	6:32
14.	The Warriors	18:47

Volume 7, *Songs for Tenor* (Chan 9610) is a collection including fourteen premiere recordings for tenor, featuring Martyn Hill and pianist Penelope Thwaites.

1.–9.	Nine settings of Rudyard Kipling (1865–1936)	31:33
10.–12.	Three settings of Robert Burns (1759–1796)	13:10
13.–16.	Four settings of the North	10:09
17.	The Power of Love (Traditional)	4:30
18.	The Twa Corbies (Traditional)	3:27
19.	A Reiver's Neck-Verse	2:16
20.	Lord Maxwell's Goodnight (Traditional)	3:38

Volume 8, *Works for Wind Orchestra 2* (Chan 9630), features Timothy Reynish and Clark Rundell conducting the Royal Northern College Wind Orchestra in nine selections including:

1.	The Power of Rome and the Christian Heart	12:06
2.	Children's March	6:48
3.	Bell Piece	5:32
4.	Blithe Bells	3:35
5.	The Immovable Do	4:07
6.	Hill Song I	14:18
7.	Hill Song II	5:05
8.	Irish Tune from County Derry	6:30
9.	Marching Song of Democracy	6:36

Volume 9, *Works for Chorus and Orchestra 3* (Chan 9653), features Susan Gritton, soprano; Pamela Helen Stephen, mezzo-soprano; Marh Tucker, tenor; Stephen Varcoe, baritone; Tim Hugh, cello; and the Joyful Company of Singers and the City of London Sinfonia under the baton of Richard Hickox. As with Volume 5, there are three premiere recordings on this disc, indicated with an *.

1.	Mock Morris	3:21
2.	The Power of Love	4:23
3.	Died For Love	1:29
4.	Love Verses from *The Song of Solomon*	6:45
5.	Shepherd's Hey	2:07
6.	Early One Morning	2:02
7.	The Three Ravens	4:04
8.	Scherzo*	1:40
9.	Youthful Rapture	5:11
10.	Randon Round (Set version)*	6:01
11.	The Merry King	4:22
12.	O Gin I Were Where Gadie Rins*	1:43
13.	Skye Boat Song	3:30
14.	Danny Deever	3:16
15.	Irish Tune from County Derry (1952)	3:36
16.	Dollar and a Half a Day	3:21
17.	Molly on the Shore	4:08

Volume 10, *Works for Pianos* (Chan 9702), is proof that Grainger's view of pianists, solo creatures as they often are, needed the experience of performing with other musicians. Few composers have produced such a body of works for more than one keyboard.

1.	Green Bushes (see *English Folk Song Suite*)	7:45
2.	Let's Dance in Green Meadow	0:47
3.	In Bristol Town	0:44
4.	English Dance	9:33
5.	Zanzibar Boat Song	4:08
6.	'The Widow's Party' March*	4:14
7.	Ye Banks and Braes O 'Bonnie Doon	2:13

8.	Jutish Medley	7:54
9.	Harvest Hymn	2:45
10.	Country Gardens	1:59
11.	Random Round	5:32
12.	The Keel-Row*	1:13
13.	The Warriors	9:19

Volume 11, *Works for Chorus and Orchestra 4* (Chan 9721), is a testament to Grainger's love for Scandinavian literature and especially the Icelandic Sagas. Grainger visited Denmark in 1922, 1925, and 1927 and recorded and notated well over 170 folk songs. It was from this wealth of material that Grainger eventually composed his series of Danish Folk Music Settings. This recording features the Danish National Radio Choir and Danish National Radio Orchestra.

1.	Fadir og Dottir (Father and Daughter)	3·02
2.	Kleine Variationen-Form	5:17
3.	A Song of Värmeland	2:51
4.	To a Nordic Princess	12:31
5.	The Merry Wedding	6:40
6.	Stalt Vesselil (Proud Veselil)	3:20
7.	The Rival Brothers	1:13
8.	Dalvisa	1:08
9.	The Crew of the Long Serpent	4:47
10.	Under en bro (Under a Bridge)	3:44
11.–14.	Danish Folk-song Suite	19:22

Volume 12, *Works for Mezzo Soprano* (Chan 9730), features Della Jones, mezzo-soprano with Penelope Thwaites, piano. Additional artists include Mark Padmore, tenor; Stephen Varcoe, baritone; and John Lavender, second piano.

13.	C. Hughes-Daffyd Y Garreg Wen (David of the White Rock) 2:08	
14.	Died for Love (Traditional)	1:42
15.	The Spring of Thyme (Traditional)	2:10
16.	Willow, Willow	2:10
17.	Near Woodstock Town	1:40
18.	Early One Morning (Traditional)	2:31
19.	In Bristol Town (Traditional)	2:29
	Four Settings from Songs of the North	
8.	Weaving Song	1:50
9.	This Is No Plaid	1:25
10.	Skye Boat Song	1:52
11.	Turn Ye To Me	2:42
12.	The Bridegroom Grat (Traditional)	1:34
13.	Lady Nairne—The Land O' the Leal	2:06
14.	Proud Vesselil (Traditional)	4:03
15.	Under A Bridge (Traditional)	3:21

16.	Hubby and Wifey (Traditional)	1:15
17.	The Lonely Desert—Man Sees the Tents of the Happy Tribes	2:47
18.	Colonial Song	5:47
19.	Kipling—The Only Son	4:05
20.	Kipling—The Love Song of Har Dyal	2:48
21.	A L Gordon—A Song of Autumn	1:34
	Five Settings of Ella Grainger	
22.	To Echo	1:37
23.	Honey Pot Bee	1:29
24.	Farewell to an Atoll	1:45
25.	Crying for the Moon	1:35
26.	Love at First Sight	1:48
27.	F Corteccia—O Glorious, Golden Era	1:43
	Percy and Ella Grainger	
28.	Little Ole with his Umbrella	2:33
29.	Variations on Handel's 'The Harmonius Blacksmith'	1:28
30.	Harvest Hymn	2:45
31.	After-word	2:58

Volume 13, *Works for Chamber Ensemble* (Chan 9746), features the Academy of St. Martin in the Fields Chamber Ensemble performing fifteen works which Grainger referred to as 'room-music' or solo instrumental chamber music. It can be placed into three main categories: original works, folk-song arrangements, and pieces that were not originally conceived for this medium but which were 'elastically' scored. Thereby allowing for a minumum scoring of three of four instruments (most usually for piano trio).

1.	Molly on the Shore	3:37
2.	My Robin is to the Greenwood Gone	4:57
3.	Shepherd's Hey	2:06
4.	Harvest Hymn	2:40
5.	Arrival Platform Humlet	3:08
6.	Handel in the Strand	4:17
	La Scandinavie (Scandinavian Suite)	15:51
7.	I Swedish Air and Dance	2:38
8.	II Song of Värmeland	1:51
9.	III Norwegian Polska	2:47
10.	IV Danish Melody	2:47
11.	V Air and Finale on Norwegian Dances	5:32
12.	The Nightingale and The Two Sisters	3:31
13.	The Maiden and the Frog	1:00
14.	The Shoemaker from Jerusalem	3:18
15.	Mock Morris	3:27
16.	The Sussex Mummers' Christmas Carol	3:40
17.	Theme and Variations	8:53
18.	Youthful Rapture	5:04
19.	Colonial Song	6:02

Volume 14, *Works for Chamber Ensemble 2* (Chan 9819), features the Academy of St Martin in the Fields Chamber Ensemble with Della Jones, mezzo-soprano, Martyn Hill, tenor, and Stephen Varcoe, baritone.

1.	Lord Peter's Stable-Boy	3:12
2.	The Shoemaker from Jerusalem	3:15
3.	Hubby and Wifey	1:18
4.	The Only Son	3:41
5.	Ye Banks and Breas O' Bonny Doon	2:36
6.	Lisbon [for wind quartet] (see *Lincolnshire Posy*)	1:23
7.	The Bridegroom Grat	1:43
8.	The Land O' the Leal	2:22
9.	Walking Tune	3:40
10.	Willow, Willow	4:18
11.	Harvest Hymn	3:04
12.	The Old Woman at the Christening	2:42
13.	The Nightingale	2:04
14.	The Two Sisters	2:30
15.	Sea Song (Sketch)	0:33
16.	Bold William Taylor	3:39
17.	The Power of Love	4:00
18.	Lord Maxwell's Goodnight	3:26
13.	Colonial Song (for mezzo-soprano, tenor, violin, cello and piano)	6:21
20.	Free Music	1:57
21.	The Twa Corbies	3:28
22.	Died for Love	3:30
23	Molly on the Shore (for string quartet)	3:30

Volume 15, *Orchestral Works 3* (Chan 9839), features the BBC Philharmonic under the baton of Richard Hickox. This collection serves as a reminder that no new compositional ideas appeared to Grainger after the death of his mother Rose in 1922. Instead, he feverishly re-worked and re-arranged existing pieces. Thus, the selections on this disc represent the result of such re-working and re-arranging.

1.	Green Bushes (see *English Folk Song Suite*)	7:19
	(Passacaglia on an English folk-tune, 1905/06 version)	
2.	Hill-Song No.2	4:52
3.	The Merry King	4:08
4.	Eastern Intermezzo (for percussion ensemble)	1:57
5.	Colonial Song (1919 version)	5:54
6.	Spoon River	4:15
7.	Lord Maxwell's Goodnight	3:19
8.	The Power of Rome and the Christian Heart	14:17
9.	The Immovable Do (The Cyphering C)	4:42
10.	Irish Tune from County Derry (County Derry Air)	5:52
11.	Ye Banks and Braes O' Bonnie Doon	2:35
12.	English Dance No. 1	10:00

Volume 16, *Works for Solo Piano 1* (Chan 9895), was recorded on April 3–5, 2000 in St. Paul's Church, Knightsbridge, London, and features Penelope Twaites as pianist.

1.	Prelude in G	2:57
2.	Prelude in C	0:47
3.	Gigue	0:51
4.	Andante con moto	3:23
5.	Klavierstück in D major	3:38
6.	Klavierstück in E major	6:44
7.	Klavierstück in A minor	5:45
8.	Klavierstück in B flat	1:38
9.	Peace	2:50
10.	Saxon Twi-Play	2:07
11.	Eastern Intermezzo	2:19
12.	English Waltz (see *English Waltz*)	5:22
13.	At Twilight	1:20
14.	Train Music	0:36
15.	Sailor's Song	2:40
16.	Walking Tune	3:44
	Three Scotch Folksongs	4:14
17.	I Will ye gang to the Hielands, Leezie Lindsay?	1:05
18.	II Mo Dighean Dubh	1:47
19.	III O gin I were where Gadie rins	1:22
20.	Scotch Strathspey and Reel	5:11
21.	Seven men from all the world	2:00
22.	Paraphrase on Tchaikovsky's Flower Waltz	7:08
23.	Irish Tune from County Derry	3:52
24.	Near Woodstock (Old English Song)	2:12
25.	In Dahomey ('Cakewalk Smasher')	4:24

Volume 17, *Works for Solo Piano 2* (Chan 9919), was recorded on March 1–3, 2001 in St. Paul's Church, Knightsbridge, London, and features Penelope Twaites performing twenty-seven additional works written and arranged for piano by Grainger.

1.	Tiger-Tiger!	1:40
2.	The Hunter in His Career	2:49
3.	The Sussex Mummers' Christmas Carol	2:51
4.	The Rival Brothers	1:15
5.	Australian Up-Country Song	1:03
6.	Harvest Hymn	3:14
7.	The Merry King (English Folksong)	4:58
8.	Lisbon [Dublin Bay] (see *Lincolnshire Posy*)	1:21
9.	Pastoral—No. 3 from *In a Nutshell*	10:06
10.	The Widow's Party	1:44

11.	Died for Love	1:59
12.	Horkstow Grange (see *Lincolnshire Posy*)	1:19
	'The Miser and His Man'—A Local Tragedy	
13.	The Brisk Young Sailor (who returned to wed his true love)	0:33
	English Folksong (see *Lincolnshire Posy*)	
14.	Hard-Hearted Barb'ra (H)Ellen	0:57
15.	Bristol Town—English Folksong	0:47
16.	Sea-Song Sketch	0:48
17.	Molly on the Shore—Irish Reel for Piano	3:33
18.	Arrival Platform Humlet—No. 1 from *In a Nutshell*	2:26
19.	Sherpherd's Hey	2:04
20.	Country Gardens	2:01
21.	Mock Morris	3:58
22.	'The Gum-Suckers' March	4:04
23.	Colonial Song	6:14
24.	The Tents of the Happy Tribes	1:15
25.	Gay but Wistful—No. 2 from *In a Nutshell*	2:43
26.	Handel in the Strand	2:49
27.	My Robin Is to the Greenwood Gone	5:01

Volume 18, *Works for Unaccompanied Chorus* (Chan 9987), features the Academy of St Martin in the Fields Chorus under the baton of Richard Hickox.

1.	My Love's in Germanie	3:49
2.	Six Dukes Went A fishin'	2:07
3.	O Mistress Mine	1:35
4.	Mary Thomson	2:42
5.	Early One Morning	2:53
6.	Irish Tune from County Derry	3:30
7.	Agincourt Song	1:34
8.	Australian Up-Country Song	1:39
9.	Recessional	3:40
10.	At Twilight	3:57
11.	The Gipsy's Wedding Day	1:35
12.	Mo Nighean Dubh (My dark-hair maiden)	4:25
13.	Ye Banks and Braes O' Bonnie Doon	2:25
14.	Soldier, Soldier	2:56
	Jungle-Book Verses	
15.	Night-Song in the Jungle	0:55
16.	Lukannon	5:32
17.	Hunting-Song of the Seeonee Pack	1:28
18.	Tiger-Tiger	0:58
19.	Near Woodstock Town	3:00
20.	Love at First Sight	2:03

CHANDOS SUMMARY

Ralph Couzens, Director of Chandos Records, points to the company's enviable reputation for comprehensive surveys of composers' works, citing the William Walton edition that was spread over twenty-three CDs. A number of key people are involved in contributing to the quality of *The Grainger Edition* such as Barry Ould, Secretary and Archivist of the Percy Grainger Society, pianist Penelope Thwaites, who was educated at Melbourne University in the 1960's and took her Grainger lecture/recital around the world, and conductor Richard Hickox who insists that the schedule be restricted to two CDs per year in order to insure that performances are of the highest possible standard. Of the investment of time and thought for the preparation of each album, Hickox states:

> We will not be cutting corners for the Grainger Edition. If Grainger says, at the front of his score, for instance, that he wants three pianos and, ideally, five celestas, we will source them because their sound will made a difference. We are determined to ensure that the Chandos Grainger Edition will be as authentic and comprehensive as possible.[1]

Barry Ould has researched most of the scores used for the Chandos project and has contributed the impressive booklet of notes that accompanies each compact disc recording. He has made several trips to White Plains, New York to visit Percy's widow, Ella, and her second husband, Stewart Manville. "They gave me lots of Grainger's musical manuscripts. I went to America with one suitcase and returned with four!" remembered Ould.[2]

Commenting about the recordings of the music, Richard Hickox said, "As far as the choral music is concerned, it is very important to get the local dialects right because they color the music so much. A Lincolnshire folk song should be sung in a proper Lincolnshire accent, not a vague Lincolnshire drawl, so we ensured that the singers were coached in the proper dialects by local people."[3] This statement brings to mind the pages that Grainger included at the end of his article, "Collecting with the Phonograph," which included a key to dialect pronunciation. "I have chosen to indicate dialect pronunciation by means of accents over vowels, rather than by 'spelling out,' because of the greater uniformity and phonetic exactness of the first-named method, and in hope that it will present a less disturbing picture to the eye than a series of unfamiliar spellings."[4]

After listening to the quality of musicianship in performance and marveling at the creativity of Percy Grainger's settings in the **Chandos Grainger Edition** CDs, one realizes the importance of this collection. How wonderful that the creativity of one individual has sparked such diligent scholarship of several of the artists and researchers mentioned above, and will continue to spark creative endeavors in the recording industry for the next few years on *The Grainger Edition* alone!

ENDNOTES

1. Ian Lace, "Percy Grainger—A Reassessment," *Fanfare* 20/4 (1997): 42.
2. Ian Lace, "Percy Grainger—A Reassessment," *Fanfare* 20/4 (1997): 40.
3. Ibid.
4. Percy Grainger, "Collecting with the Phonograph," *Journal of the Folk-Song Society* 3 (1908–09): 167.

CHAPTER FOUR

FOLK SONGS USED IN THE WIND BAND MASTERWORKS OF HOLST, VAUGHAN WILLIAMS, AND GRAINGER

Throughout this book, emphasis has been placed on the power of the text to shape an appropriate interpretation of instrumental music containing folk song sources. In order to understand the relationship, one must remember the role of the text from an historical perspective. The ballad style, viewed as far back as the sixteenth century, involved a process by which the poet set words to music. Essentially, these works were poems that were sung. The audience may have ranged from a small group to the entire culture, and the texts of these poems spoke of the life experiences of the people. As a result, the poems were highly charged from an emotional standpoint. Mostly narrative in form, the poems made reference to rituals, the very communal rituals that held a community together.[1]

In preparing a textual analysis of the folk songs that comprise the repertoire found in this book, some interesting similarities were discovered. The following table represents a summary of the main thematic ideas presented in the folks songs used in the works selected for analysis. The thematic ideas have been arranged in alphabetical order with a number indicated in parenthesis if the thematic idea was found in more than one of the folk songs.

Often, more than one thematic idea is presented in the course of reading the many verses of the text. For this reason, one will note additional separate entries on the following table.

THEMATIC IDEAS OF FOLK SONGS USED IN THIS STUDY
(Thematic Ideas used in more than one song are noted)

Absent Lover (3)	Growing Up	River Banks (2)
Admiral Benbow	Harry	Roving
Beauty (Fair Maiden) (2)	Horkstow Grange	Rufford Park
Betsy	John (2)	Sailor (2)
Blacksmith	Johnny	Sea
Bonnie (Bonny) Boy	Lamenting (2)	Seventeen (years of age)
Captain (2)	Lazarus	Soldier
Caroline	Lisbon	Spain
Cavaliers	Lord Melbourne	Spring Evening
Claudy Banks	Lost Lady	Sunday
Courtship (3)	Marriage (3)	Swansea Town
Diverus	May Evening	Thwarted Love (2)
Drowning Sailor	May Morning (4)	Tree
Duke of Marlborough	Miser (and his Servant)	Troy
Farewell to a Lover (3)	Month of May (2)	Undying Love
Farmer (and his Son)	Morning Dew	Village Song (2)
Field of Battle	Nancy (2)	Walking (4)
France (2)	Poachers	War Song (2)
Gardens (4)	Polly (2)	Wednesday
Germany (2)	Portsmouth	William
Going off to Sea (7)	Queen	Winter Night
Green Bushes	Rich Man/Poor Man	Young Maid
Greensleeves	Riding a Horse	

While it is obvious that several of the folk songs make direct references to precise geographical locations, many others speak of the reoccurring themes of beauty, love, and courtship as well as the plight of the men who go off to battle (land or sea) and the lamentations of the women they leave behind. Of notable interest are the themes surrounding the month of May as well as those of May mornings and evenings. Absorbed in our lives of modern convenience, it is easy to forget just how harsh the winter months must have been on the people of earlier times. The coming of spring has been traditionally marked with various types of spring festivals including one marking the first day of May. It is little wonder, then, that nine of the folk songs make thematic reference to May.

The pages that follow contain complete texts to all folk songs researched in this publication. It has been designed as a reference section, thus allowing the wind band conductor to easily identify where each folk song is located within the band master-work. Each tells a story, and the stories provide the material to inspire a powerful visual imagery among instrumentalists who are given the opportunity to learn more about the music they are performing.

ENDNOTES

1. Professor Emeritus Charles J. Scanzello of Kutztown University of PA, interview by author, 6 July 1998, Kutztown, PA.

SWANSEA TOWN / Second Suite in F Mvt. I meas. 46–110

Oh! Farewell to you my Nancy
ten thousand times adieu,
I'm bound to cross the ocean, girl,
once more to part with you;
Once more to part from you, fine girl,
you're the girl that I adore,
But still I live in hopes to see old Swansea Town once more.

Oh! It's now that I am out at sea,
and you are far behind,
Kind letters I will write to you
of the secrets of my mind;
The secrets of my mind, fine girl,
you're the girl that I adore,
But still I live in hopes to see old Swansea Town once more.

Oh! Now the storm is rising,
I can see it coming it on,
The night so dark as anything
we cannot see the moon.
Our good old ship, she is toss'd aft,
our rigging is all tore,
But still I live in hopes to see old Swansea Town once more.

Oh! it's now the storm is over
and we are safe, are safe on shore,
We'll drink strong drinks and brandies to the girls,
To the girls that we adore, fine girls,
we'll make, we'll make this tavern roar,
And when our money is all gone
we'll go to sea for more.

CLAUDY BANKS / Second Suite in F Mvt. I meas. 111–159

As I roved out one evening all in the month of May,
Down by the Banks of Claudy I carelessly did stray,
There I beheld a young maid in sorrow did complain,
Lamenting of her true Love who had crossed the raging main.
    Io, Io, he is my darling boy,
    He is the darling of my heart upon the walls of Troy.

I steppéd up unto her and gave her a great suprise.
I won she did not know me, for I was in disguise.
I said, "My pretty fair maid, my joy and heart's delight,
How far do you mean to wander this dark and dreary night?"
     Io, Io, etc.

It's on the Banks of Claudy I wish you would me show
Take on a fair young maid who has nowhere to go,
For I am in search of a young man, young Johnny is his name,
And on the Banks of Claudy I hear he does remain."
     Io, Io, etc.

"This is the Banks of Claudy, on them you now do stand,
Do not believe young Johnny, for he's a false young man.
Do not believe young Johnny, he will not meet you here,
Through the green woods you may tarry, no danger you may fear."
     Io, Io, etc.

"Oh if my Johnny were here to-night, he would keep me from all harm,
But he's on the field of battle and in his uniform.
He's on the field of battle, all danger he does defy,
Like the royal king of honour upon the walls of Troy.
     Io, Io, etc.

It's six long months, and better, since my Johnny left the shore
To cross the raging ocean where thundering billows roar,
To cross the raging ocean for honour and for fame."
"I heard the ship was wrecked upon the coasts of Spain."
     Io, Io, etc.

As soon as she heard this, she fell in deep despair,
A-wringing of her lily-white hands and a-tearing of her hair,
Saying, "If my Johnny's drownded, no other man I'll take,
Through lonesome woods and valleys will I wander for his sake."
     Io, Io, etc.

As soon as he had heard this, no longer could he stand;
he flew into her arms, saying, "Betsy, I'm the man."
Saying, "Betsy, I'm the young man who caused your grief and pain,
And since we've met on Claudy's fair Banks, we never will part again."
     Io, Io, etc.

I LOVE MY LOVE / Second Suite in F Mvt. II

Abroad as I was walking, one evening in the spring,
I heard a maid in Bedlam so sweetly for to sing;
Her chains she rattled with her hands, and thus replied she:
"I love my love, because I know my love loves me!"

Oh! cruel were his parents who sent my love to sea,
And cruel was the ship that bore my love from me;
Yet I love his parents since they're his although they've ruined me:
"I love my love, because I know my love loves me!"

"With straw I'll weave a garland, I'll weave it very fine;
With roses, lilies, daises, I'll mix the eglantine;
And I'll present it to my love when he returns from sea.
For I love my love, because I know my love loves me."

Just as she sat there weeping, her love he came on land,
Then, hearing she was in Bedlam, he ran straight out of hand;
He flew into her snow-white arms, and thus replied he:
"I love my love, because I know my love loves me!"

She said: "My love don't frighten me; are you my love or no?"
"O yes, my dearest Nancy, I am your love, also
I am returned to make amends for all your injury;
"I love my love, because I know my love loves me!"

So now these two are married, and happy may they be,
Like turtle-doves together, in love and unity.
All pretty maids with patience wait, that have got loves at sea;
"I love my love, because I know my love loves me!"

THE SONG OF THE BLACKSMITH / Second Suite in F Mvt. III

Kang kang kang ki ki kang
kang kang ki ki kang kang

For the blacksmith courted me,
nine months and better;
And first he won my heart,
till he wrote to me a letter.
With his hammer in his hand,
for he strikes so mighty and clever,
He makes the sparks to fly
all round his middle.

GREENSLEEVES / Second Suite in F Mvt. IV meas. 58–88

Alas my love you do me wrong,
To cast me off discourteously;
And I have loved you for so long,
Delighting in your company.

Chorus. Greensleeves was all my joy,
Greensleeves was my delight,
Greensleeves was my heart of gold,

And who but my lady Greensleeves.

I long have waited at your hand
To do your bidding as your slave,
And waged, have I, both life and land
Your love and affection for to have.

Greensleeves…

If you intend thus to distain
It does the more enrapture me,
And even so, I will remain
Your lover in captivity.

Greensleeves…

Alas, my love, that yours should be
A heart of faithless vanity,
So here I mediate alone
Upon your insincerity.

Greensleeves…

Ah, Greensleeves, now farewell, adieu,
To God I pray to prosper thee,
For I remain thy lover true,
Come once again and be with me.

Greensleeves…

SEVENTEEN COME SUNDAY / English Folk Song Suite Mvt. I meas. 4–30

As I rose up one May morning,
One May morning so early,
I overtook a pretty fair maid
Just as the sun was dawning.
    with me rue rum ray,
    fother diddle ay,
    wok fol air diddle i-do.

Her stockings white and her boots were bright
And her buckles shone like silver,
She had a dark and rolling eye
And her hair hung down her shoulders.
    With me…

Where are you going, my pretty fair maid,
Where are you going my honey?
She answered me right cheerfully:
On an errand for my mammy.
    With me…

How old are you, my pretty fair maid,
How old are you, my honey?
She answered me right cheerfully:
I am seventeen come Sunday.
  With me...

Will you take a man, my sweet pretty maid,
Will you take a man, my honey?
She answered me right cheerfully:
I dare not for my mammy.
  With me...

If you will come to my mammy's house
When the moon is shining clearly;
You come down, I'll let you in
And my mammy shall not hear me.
  With me...

And now I am with my soldier lad
Where the wars are quite alarming;
The drum and fife is my delight
And a merry man in the morning.
  With me. . .

PRETTY CAROLINE / English Folk Song Suite Mvt. I meas. 32–63 & 97–129

One morning in the month of May,
How lovely shone the sun,
All on the banks of daiscs gay
There sat a lovely one.
She did appear as goddess fair
And her dark brown hair did shine
It shaded her neck and bosom
Of my pretty Caroline.

LAZARUS / English Folk Song Suite Mvt. I meas. 64–97

As it fell out upon one day,
Rich Diverus he made a feast;
And he invited all his friends,
And gentry of the best.
And it fell out upon one day,
Poor Lazarus he was so poor,
He came and laid him down and down,
Ev'n down at Diverus' door.

So Lararus laid him down and down,
Ev'n down at Diverus' door;

"Some meat, some drink, brother Diverus,
Do bestow upon the poor."
"Thou are none of mine, brother Lazarus,
Lying begging at my door,
No meat, no drink will I give thee,
Nor bestow upon the poor."

Then Lararus laid him down and down,
Ev'n down at Diverus' wall;
"Some meat, some drink, brother Diverus,
Or surely starve I shall."
"Thou art none of mine, brother Lazarus,
Lying begging at my wall,
No meat, no drink will I give thee,
And therefore starve thou shall."

Then Lararus laid him down and down,
Ev'n down at Diverus' gate;
"Some meat, some drink, brother Diverus,
For Jesus Christ his sake."
"Thou art none of mine, brother Lazarus,
Lying begging at my gate,
No meat, no drink will I give thee,
For Jesus Christ his sake."

Then Diverus sent his merry men all,
To whip poor Lazarus away;
They had not the power to whip one whip,
But threw their whips away.
Then Diverus sent out his hungry dogs,
To bite poor Lazarus away;
They had not power to bite one bite,
But licked his sores away.

And it fell out upon one day,
Poor Lazarus he sickened and died;
There came to angels out of heaven,
His soul thereto to guide.
"Rise up, rise up, brother Lazarus,
And come along with me,
There is a place prepared in heaven,
For to sit upon an angel's knee."

And it fell out upon one day,
Rich Diverus sickened and died;
There came two serpents out of hell
His soul thereto to guide.
"Rise up, rise up, brother Diverus,

And come along with me;
There is a place prepared in hell,
For to sit upon a serpent's knee."

MY BONNIE, BONNIE BOY / English Folk Song Suite Mvt. II meas. 2–40 & 77–97

I once loved a boy, a bonnie, bonnie, boy,
I loved him, I'll vow and protest;
I loved him so well, and so very, very well,
That I built him a berth on my breast,
That I built him a berth on my breast.

T'was up the green valley and down the green grove
Like one that was troubled in mind,
She whooped and she halloed and she played upon her pipe,
But no bonnie boy she could find,
But no bonnie boy she could find.

She looked up high, and she looked down low,
The sun did shine wonderful warm;
Whom should she spy there but her bonnie, bonnie boy,
So close in another girl's arms,
So close in another girl's arms.

I passed him by, on him ne'er cast an eye,
Though he stretched forth his lily-white hand,
For I thought he'd been bound to love but one,
So I would not obey his command,
So I would not obey his command.

The girl that was loved of my bonnie, bonnie boy,
I am sure she is greatly to blame,
For many's the night he has robbed me of rest,
But he never shall do it again,
But he never shall do it again.

My bonnie, bonnie boy is gone over the sea,
I fear I shan't see him again;
But were I to have him, or were I to not
I will think of him once now and then,
I will think of him once now and then.

GREEN BUSHES / English Folk Song Suite Mvt. II meas. 43–76

As I was a-walking one morning in May
For to hear the birds whistle and the nightingales sing,
I sawed a young damsel, so sweet-a-lie sang she
Down by the green bushes when she thinks to meet me.

I'll buy you fine beaver and fine silken gowns,
I'll buy you fine petticoats flounced down to the ground,
If you will prove loyal and constant to me,
And forsake your own true love and get married to me.

I don't want your beaver nor fine silken hose,
I was never so poor as to marry for clothes,
But if you will prove loyal and constant to me,
I'll forsake my own true love and get married to thee.

Come let us be going, kind sir, if you please,
Come let us be going from under the trees,
For my true love is coming down yonder I see,
Down among the green bushes where he thinks to meet me.

O when he came there and he found she was gone,
He stood like a lambkin that was all forlorn.
She's gone with some other, she's quite forsaken me,
Down among the green bushes where she thinks to meet me.

Now I'll be like a schoolboy and spend my time in play,
For I never was so false deluded away.
She's gone with some other which grieves me full sore,
So adieu to the green bushes, 'tis time to give o'er.

BLOW AWAY THE MORNING DEW / English Folk Song Suite Mvt. III
meas. 5–28 & 45–68

There was a farmer's son
Kept sheep all on the hill;
And he walked out one May morning,
To see what he could kill.
     Chorus. And sing blow away the morning dew,
       The dew, and the dew,
       Blow away the morning dew,
       How sweet the winds do blow.

He look-ed high, he look-ed low,
He cast an under look:
And there he saw a fair pretty maid
Beside the watery brook.

Cast over me my mantel fair
And pin it o'er my gown;
And, if you will, take hold my hand,
And I will be your own.

If you come down to my father's house,
Which is wall-ed all around;

There you shall have a kiss from me,
And twenty thousand pound.

He mounted on a milk-white steed,
And she upon another:
And then they rode along the lane,
Like sister and like brother.

As they were riding on alone,
They saw some pooks of hay.
O is not this a very pretty place
For the boys and girls to play?

But when they came to her father's gate,
So nimble she popped in:
And said: There is a fool without
And here's the maid within.

We have a flower in our garden,
We call it Marygold:
And if you will not when you may,
You shall not when you wolde.

HIGH GERMANY / English Folk Song Suite Mvt. III meas. 29–44

O Polly, Love, O Polly, the rout has now begun
And we must march away at the beating of the drum:
Go dress yourself all in your best and come along with me,
I'll take you to the cruel wars in High Germany.

O Harry, O Harry, you mind what I do say,
My feet they are so tender I cannot march away,
And besides, my dearest Harry, though I'm not in love with thee.
How am I fit for cruel wars in High Germany?

I'll buy you a horse, my Love, and on it you shall ride,
And all my heart's delight shall be riding by your side;
We'll call at every ale-house, and drink when we are dry,
So quickly on the road, my Love, we'll marry by and by.

O cursed were the cruel wars that ere they should rise
And out of merry England press many a lad likewise!
They pressed young Harry from me, likewise my brothers three,
And sent them to the cruel wars in High Germany.

THE TREE SO HIGH / English Folk Song Suite Mvt. III meas. 73–88

The trees that do grow high and the leaves they do grow green,
The time is gone and past, my love, when you and I had seen.

One cold winter's night, my love, when you and I alone had been.
The bonny lad is young but he's growing.

I sent him to the college for one year or two,
And perhaps in the time, my love, he then will do for you.
We'll buy him white ribbons to tie round his bonny waist,
To let the ladies know that he's married.

I went unto the college and looked over the wall.
I saw four and twenty gentlement s-playing there at the ball.
They would not let him go for her true love she did call,
Because he was a young man and a-growing.

I made my love a shroud of the fine holland brown,
And every stitch I put in it the tears they will run down.
And there I'll sit and mourne his fate until the day I die,
But I'll watch all on his child while it's growing.

For now my love is dead and in his grave doth lie,
The green grass was growing over him so very high,
Saying: Once I had a sweetheart but now I have never a one,
For he was to me my own true love for ever.

THE TREE SO HIGH (VARIANT) / English Folk Song Suite Mvt. III
meas. 73–88

The trees that do grow high
And the leaves they do grow green;
The time is gone and past, my love,
That you and I have seen.
It's a cold winter's night, my love,
When you and I must lie alone.
The bonny lad is young, but he's growing.

O father, dear father,
I've feared you've done my harm,
You've married me to a boy
And I fear he is too young.
O daughter, dearest daughter,
And if you stay at home and wait along of me
A lady you shall be while he's growing.

We'll send him to the college
For one year or two,
And perhaps in the time, my love,
A man he may grow.
I will buy you a bunch of white ribbons
To tie round his bonny, bonny waist
To let the ladies know that he's married.

At the age of sixteen,
O he was a marricd man;
At the age of seventeen
She brought to him a son;
At the age of eighteen, my love,
O his grave was growing green,
And that soon put an end of his growing.

I made my love a shroud
Of the holland so fine;
And every stitch she put in it
The tears came trickling down.
O once I had a sweetheart,
But now I have got never a one,
So fare you well, my own true love, for ever.

Hc is dead and buried
And is the churchyard laid.
The green grass is over him
So very, very thick.
O once I had a sweetheart,
But now I have got never a one,
So fare you well, my own true love, for ever.

JOHN BARLEYCORN / English Folk Song Suite Mvt. III meas. 89–113

There was three men come from the North
The vic'try for to try
Then these three men did vow and declare
John Barleycorn should die
To my rite folle rol lol liddle for le rol
Rite fol le rol li day.

ADMIRAL BENBOW (BENBOW, THE BROTHER TAR'S SONG) /
Sea Songs meas. 33–48

Come, all you sailors bold,
Lend an ear, lend an ear,
Come all you sailors bold, lend an ear:
It's of our Admiral's fame,
Brave Benbow call'd by name,
How he fought on the main
You shall hear, you shall hear.

Brave Benbow he set sail
For to fight, for to fight,
Brave Benbow he set sail for to fight:

Brave Benbow he set sail,
With a fine and pleasant gale,
But his Captains they tutr'd tail
In a fright, in a fright.

Says Kirby unto Wade,
"I will run, I will run,"
Says Kirby unto Wade, "I will run, I will run:
I value not disgrace,
Nor the losing of my place,
My enemies I'll not face
With a gun, with a gun."

'Twas the Ruby and Noah's Ark
Fought the French, fought the French,
'Twas the Ruby and Noah's Ark fought the French:
And there was ten in all,
Poor souls they fought them all,
They valued them not at all,
Nor their noise, nor their noise.

It was our Admiral's lot
With a chain shot, with a chain shot,
It was our Admiral's lot with a chain shot:
Our Admiral lost his legs,
And to his men he begs,
"Fight on, my boys," he says,
" 'Tis my lot, 'tis my lot."

While the surgeon dress'd his wounds,
Thus he said, thus he said,
While the surgeon dress'd his wounds thus he said:
"Let my cradle now in haste
On the quarter-deck be plac'd,
That my enemies I may face
Till I'm dead, till I'm dead."

And there bold Benbow lay
Crying out, crying out,
And there bold Benbow lay crying out:
"Let us tack about once more,
We'll drive them to their own shore,
I value not half a score,
Nor their noise, nor their noise."

PORTSMOUTH / Sea Songs meas. 74–106

The dreaded hour, my dear love,
Comes to us at last,

Yet I, by ling'ring here, love,
Hold the moments fast.
In spite of all I'll cherish
A fix'd and lasting joy,
A dream to bright to perish,
Time will not destroy.

Vain thought! The moments fly, love,
All are nearly gone;
Alas! Too soon shall I, love,
Find myself alone.
But still my eyes to seek thee
Will wildly gaze around:
Hard heart, will nothing break thee?
Art with iron bound?

Nay, do not bid me hope, love,
Hope I cannot bear;
Nay, rather let me cope, love,
Boldly with despair.
Should thoughts that may deceive me
Within my heart be nurs'd?
No, leave me, dearest leave me,
Now I know the worst.

LISBON / Lincolnshire Posy Mvt. 1

'Twas on one Whit-sun Wednesday
The fourteenth day of May;
We untied our anchor
And so we sailed away
Where the sun do shine most glorious,
To Lisbon we are bound,
Where the hills and hills are dainted
With pretty maidens round.

There I beheld a damsel,
All in her bloom of years,
Making her full lamentation,
Her eyes did flow with tears.
"Fare thee well my best time lover,
To thee it is well known.
So marry me sweet William
And leave me not alone."

"O no, my dearest Polly,
Pray do not go with me,
Where the soldiers they lay bleeding,

It is a dismal sight;
Where the fifes and drum are beating
To drown the dismal cry,
So stay at home dear Polly,
And do not go with I.

"If I should meet at pretty girl
That's proper tall and gay,
If I should take a fancy to her,
Polly what should you say?
Would you not be offended?"
"O no! my lover true
I'd stand aside sweet William,
While she go along with you.

"Pray do not talk of danger
For love is my desire,
To see you in the battle
And there to spend your time;
I will travel through France and Spain,
All for to be your bride,
And within the field of battle
I will lay down by your side."

HORKSTOW GRANGE / Lincolnshire Posy Mvt. II

In Horkstow Grange there lived an old miser,
You all do know him as I've heard say.
It's him and his man (that was) named John Bowlin'
They fell out one market day.

> Pity them who see him suffer,
> Pity poor old Steeleye Span;
> John Bowlin's deeds they will be remembered;
> Bowlin's deeds at Horkstow Grange.

With a blackthorn stick John Bowlin' struck him,
Oftens had threatened him before;
John Bowlin' turned round all in a passion,
He knocked old Steeleye onto t'floor.

> Pity them who see him suffer, [etc.]

John Bowlin' struck him quite sharply;
It happened to be on a market day,
Old Steeleye swore with all his vengeance,
He would swear his life away.

> Pity them who see him suffer, [etc.]

RUFFORD PARK POACHERS / Lincolnshire Posy Mvt. III

They say that forty gallant poachers there was a mess;
They'ad often been attacked when the number it was less.

Chorus. So poacher bold, as I unfold, keep up your gallant heart,
And think about those poachers bold, that night at Rufford Park.

A buck or doe, believe it so, a pheasant or an 'are
Was sent on earth for ev'ry one quite equal for to share.

So poacher bold, as I unfold, keep up your gallant heart,
And think about those poachers bold, that night at Rufford Park.

The keepers they begun to fight, With stones and with their flails,
But when the poachers they started to fight, They quickly turned their tails.

So poacher bold, as I unfold, keep up your gallant heart,
And think about those poachers bold, that night at Rufford Park.

[The next verse, of which Mr. Taylor could not remember the form, tells of a head-keeper, named Roberts, being killed. Mr. Taylor said the song is founded on fact. P.A.G.]

THE BRISK YOUNG SAILOR / Lincolnshire Posy Mvt. IV

A fair maiden walkin' all in her garden,
A brisk young sailor she chanced to spy;
He skipped up to her thinking to woo her,
Cried thus: "Fair maid, can you fancy I?"
She tells him that she has a true love of her own,
who has been away seven years.
"But seven more I will wait of him,
For if he's alive he'll return to me."

The sailor then draws forth the "true love token,"
upon viewing this she falls upon in a faint.
Then he took her up all in his arms,
And gave her kisses one, two a three.
"Here stands thy true and faithful sailor,
Who has just returned to marry thee."

THE DUKE OF MARLBOROUGH / Lincolnshire Posy Mvt. V

I am an Englishman by my birth,
And Marlborough is my name,
In Devonshire I drew my breath,
That place of noted fame;
I was beloved by all my men,
Kings and Princes likewise,

Though many towns I often took,
I did the world surprise.

King Charles the Second I did serve,
To face our foes in France,
And at the battle of Ramilies
We boldly did advance;
The sun was down, the earth did shine,
So loudly did I cry:
Fight on, my brave boys, for England—
We'll conquer or we'll nobly die.

Now we have gained the victory,
And bravely kept the field,
We've took a number of prisoners,
And forced them to yield.
That very day my horse was shot,
All by a musket ball,
 As I was mounting up again,
My aide-de-camp did fall.

Now on a bed of sickness lay,
I am resigned to die;
Yet generals, and champions bold,
Stand true as well as I:
Take no bribes, stand true to you colours,
And fight with courage bold;
I have led my men thro' fire and smoke,
But ne'er was bribed with gold.

LORD MELBOURNE / Lincolnshire Posy Mvt. V

I am an Englishman born by birth,
Lord Melbourne is my name,
In Devonshire I first drew breath,
That place of noted fame.
I was beloved by all my men,
By kings and princes likewise;
I never failed in anything,
But one great victory.

Then good Queen Ann sent us on board,
To Flendre we did go;
We'd left the banks of Newfoundland
To face our daring foe.
We'd climed those lofty 'idells away
With broken guns shields likewise,
And all those famous towns we took,

To all the world's surprise.

King Charles the second we did reserve,
To face our foaming France,
And to the battle of Elements
We boldly did advance.
The sun was down, the earth did shake,
And I so loud did cry:
"Fight on, my lads, for Old England's sake,
We'll gain the field, or die.

And now this glorious victory's won,
So boldly keep the field;
When prisoners in great numbers took,
Which forced our foe to yield.
That very day my horse was shot,
All by a canon ball;
As soon as I got up again,
My head in camp did fall.

Now on a bed of sickness lie,
I am resigned to die.
You generals all and champions bold,
Stand true as well as I:
Stand to your men, take them on board,
And fight with courage bold;
I have led my men through smoke and fire,
But now to death must yield.

THE LOST LADY FOUND / Lincolnshire Posy Mvt. VI

'Twas down in a valley a fair maid did dwell,
She lived with her uncle, as all knew full well,
'Twas down in the valley. Where violets are gay,
Three gypsies betrayed her and stole her away.

Long time she'd been missing and could not be found,
Her uncle, he searched the country around,
Till he came to her trustee, between hope and fear,
The trustee made answer "She has not been here."

The trustee spake up with a courage so bold,
"I fear she's been lost for the sake of her gold;
So we'll have life for life, sir," the trustee did say,
"We shall send you to prison, and there you shall stay."

There was a young squire that loved her so,
Oft times to the schoolhouse together they did go;

"I'm afraid she is murdered; so great is my fear,
If I'd wings like a dove I would fly to my dear!"

He travelled through England, through France and through Spain,
He ventured his life on the watery main;
Till he came to a house where he lodged for a night,
And in that same house was his own heart's delight.

When she saw him, she knew him, and flew to his arms,
She told him her grief while he gazed on her charms
"How came you to Dublin, my dearest, I pray?"
"Three gypsies betrayed me, and stole me away."

"Your uncle's in England; in prison doth lie,
And for your sweet sake is condemned for to die."
"Carry me to old England, my dearest," she cried;
"One thousand I'll give you, and will be your bride."

When she came to old England, her uncle to see,
The cart it was under the high gallows tree.
"Oh, pardon! Oh, pardon! Oh, pardon! I crave!
Don't you see I'm alive, your dear life for to save?"

Then straight from the gallows they led him away,
The bells they did ring, and the music did play;
Every house in the valley with mirth did resound
As soon as they heard the lost lady was found.

CHAPTER FIVE 🖋

FOLK SONG SOURCES

The following table presents a complete listing of the folk song sources in an indexed format for easy reference. The folk songs are divided according to their use in each wind band masterwork. Information pertaining to the collector/composer/arranger/folk singer is provided in the second column. An abbreviated source list is provided in column three with a full listing of the sources at the end of the table.

From a theory/analysis point of view, column four provides the original key or mode for each folk song with the entry in column five showing any changes in key or mode that were used in the wind band masterworks. Speaking about the modes and scales, folk song collector/arranger Cecil J. Sharp once said:

> English folk tunes are cast in the dorian, phrygian, mixolydian, aeolian, and ionian (major) modes, and occasionally in the minor. Personally, I have never recovered an English folk tune in the minor scale, and very few have been recorded by other collectors. Minor folk airs are, no doubt, aeolian airs that have been modernized by the addition of the leading note... The cultivated musician cannot rid himself of the notion that a scale with a minor seventh is fundamentally false, and conflicts with natural law. When, therefore, he is confronted with folk tunes containing flatted sevenths he hastily concludes, either that they have been wrongly recorded, or that they are the ignorant corruptions of rude singers.[1]

In comparing Cecil Sharp's statements with the folk song index that follows, one can see the predominance of the Dorian, Aeloian, and Ionian (Major) modes with a few instances of the Mixolydian mode. In the case of *Rufford Park Poachers*, Grainger set the piece in G Melodic Minor, based on his phonograph recording of Joseph Taylor, who sang it in F#. In the case of *Lord Melbourne*, Grainger expanded the original setting in D Dorian to include notes in the minor scale as well in his treatment of the fifth movement.

ENDNOTES

1. Cecil J. Sharp, rev. ed. Maud Karpeles, *English Folk Song: Some Conclusions* (Belmont, CA: Wadsworth Publishing Co. Inc., 1965), 68.

Index of Folk Songs

Title	Collector/Composer Arranger/Singer	Source	Original Key	Wind Key
Second Suite in F				
Glorishears (Morris Dance)	Sharp/MacIlwaine	NOV	D Major	F Major
Swansea Town	Gustav Holst	CUR	D Major	F Major
Claudy Banks	Sung by Frederick White	FSJ v3	E Aeolian	B♭ Dorian
I Love My Love	Gustav Holst	CUR	F Dorian	F Dorian
I'll Love My Love	Sung by J. Boaden, Esq.	FSJ v2	D Dorian	F Dorian
Song of the Blacksmith	Gustav Holst	CUR	G Major	F Major
Dargason	Traditional	PMT	E♭ Major	F Major
Greensleeves	Traditional		E Dorian	G Dorian

Title	Collector/Composer Arranger/Singer	Source	Original Key	Wind Key
English Folk Song Suite				
Seventeen Come Sunday	Sung by Kathleen Williams	CSC	E Dorian	F Dorian
Pretty Caroline	Sung by Shadrack Clifford	CSC	D Major	A♭ Major
Lazarus	Lucy Broadwood	ECS	E Dorian	F Dorian
My Bonnie, Bonnie Boy	Lucy Broadwood	ECS	D Dorian	F Dorian
Green Bushes	Sung by James Bale	CSC	G Dorian	F Dorian
Green Bushes	Cecil J. Sharp	EFS	F Dorian	F Dorian
Blow Away The Morning Dew	Cecil J. Sharp	FSS	G Major	B♭ Major
High Germany	Sung by Mrs. Lock	FSS	D Aeolian	G Aeolian
The Tree So High	Cecil J. Sharp	CSC	G Aeolian	C Aeolian
John Barleycorn	Cecil J. Sharp	FSJv3	C Major	E♭ Major
Sea Songs				
Princess Royal	Lionel Bacon	HMD	G Major	A♭ Major
Admiral Benbow	WilliamChappell	PMT	A Minor	C Minor
Portsmouth	William Chappell	PMT	E♭ Major	D♭ Major

Title	Collector/Composer Arranger/Singer	Source	Original Key	Wind Key
Lincolnshire Posy				
Dublin Bay Sketch	Percy Grainger	PGM	C Mixolydian	A♭ Mixolydian
Lisbon Piano Score	Percy Grainger	PGM	C Mixolydian	A♭ Mixolydian
Dublin Bay Instr. Sketches	Percy Grainger	PGM	F Mixolydian	A♭ Mixolydian
Lisbon	Sung by Mrs. Lock	FSJv2	D Dorian	A♭ Mixolydian
Horkstow Grange	Percy Grainger	PGM	A Major	D♭ Major
Rufford Park Poachers	Sung by Joseph Taylor	FSJ v3	G Mel. Minor	Fm/Cm
The Brisk Young Sailor	Percy Grainger	PGM	C Major	B♭ Major
The Duke of Malborough	Sung by Mr. H. Burstow	FSJv1	C Mixolydian	D Minor
Lord Melbourne	Sung by George Wray	FSJ v3	D Dorian	D Minor
The Lost Lady Found	Sung by Mrs. Hill	FSJ v2	D Dorian	D Dorian
The Lost Lady Found Sketches	Percy Grainger	PGM	D Dorian	D Dorian
Molly on the Shore				
Temple Hill	Charles Villiers Stanford	CPC	G Major	A♭ Major

Title	Collector/Composer Arranger/Singer	Source	Original Key	Wind Key
Molly on the Shore	Charles Villiers Stanford	CPC	G Major	A♭ Major

SOURCES:

CPC	Complete Petrie Collection of Ancient Irish Music
CSC	Cecil Sharp's Collection of English Folksongs
CUR	J. Curwen & Sons, Ltd.
ECS	English Country Songs
EFS	One Hundred English Folk Songs
ETS	English Traditional Folk Songs And Carols
FSJv1	Journal Of The English Folk Song Society (Vol. 1)
FSJv2	Journal Of The English Folk Song Society (Vol. 2)
FSJv3	Journal Of The English Folk Song Society (Vol. 3)
FSS	Folk Songs From Somerset
HMD	Handbook Of Morris Dances
NOV	Novello & Company, Ltd.
PGM	Manuscripts Of Percy Grainger (Library Of Congress)
PMT	Popular Music Of The Olden Time

APPENDIX A

FROM THE PHONOGRAPH CYLINDER COLLECTION IN THE GRAINGER MUSEUM

The following list of cylinders has been made available through the courtesy of Dr. Kay Dreyfus, Curator of the Grainger Museum, The University of Melbourne. While the original fifteen page list includes the entire collection of cylinders from Grainger's work in the field, the following list highlights those recordings which relate to this particular study.

Box #	Cyl. #	Description/ Title	Date	Performers Location	Condition	Other Sources
13–24	14	John Bowlin' [Harkstow Grange] Melody no. 288	4-8-06		Fair–Poor Fungal Damage	Disc15B LEA4050
25–36	33	'Wray Lrd Melbourne Melody no. 143	28-7-06	George Wray Brigg	Fair–Slight Fungal Damage	Disc21B LEA4050
25–36	34	'Wray Lrd Melbourne Melody no. 143 2nd ver.	28-7-06	George Wray Brigg	Fair–Poor Fungal Damage	Disc21B LEA4050

Box #	Cyl. #	Description/ Title	Date	Performers Location	Condition	Other Sources
25–36	35	Lord Melbourne Melody no. 143	28-7-06	G. Gouldthorpe Brigg	Fair–Poor Fungal Damage	Disc22A LEA4050
25–36	36	'Wray Lord M. 3rd ver. Melody no. 143	28-7-06	George Wray Brigg	Fair–Slight Fungal Damage	Disc22A LEA4050
49–60	49	The Lost Lady Found Mel. no. 44 I'm Seventeen Come Sunday #125	31-7-06	Fred Atkinson	Fair–Poor Fungal Damage	Disc26A
49–60	50	The Lost Lady Found Mel. no. 44 Three Gipsies [Lost Lady Found]	31-7-06	Fred Atkinson	Fair–Slight Fungal Damage	Disc26A
61–72	68	Rufford Pk Poachers Mel. no. 117 I'm Seventeen Come Sunday #130	4-8-06	Joseph Taylor	Poor–Fungal Damage	Disc32B LEA4050
61–72	69	'Dean Lisbon 1st rec Melody no. 7	25-5-08	Mr. Dean [Deene] Brigg Workhouse	Poor–Fungal Damage	Disc33A/B
61–72	70	'Dean Lisbon 2nd rec Melody no. 7	25-5-08	Mr. Dean Brigg Union	Fair–Slight Fungal Damage	Disc33A/B

Box #	Cyl. #	Description/ Title	Date	Performers Location	Condition	Other Sources
85–96	93	'Mrs Thompson The brisk young sailor Mel. no. 121	25-5-08	Mrs. Thompson Barrow-on-Humber	Poor–Fungal Damage	Disc41A
85–96	94	'Mrs Thompson 2nd cyl The brisk young sailor Mel. no. 121	25-5-08	Mrs. Thompson Barrow-on-Humber	Poor–Slight Damage	Disc 41A

APPENDIX B

FROM THE REEL-TO-REEL TAPE COLLECTION IN THE LIBRARY OF CONGRESS

The following list of 7″ reel-to-reel tapes has been made available through the courtesy of Jennifer Cutting, Archivist in the Folklife Reading Room, The Library of Congress. While the original eight page list includes the entire collection of recordings from Grainger's work in the field, the following list highlights those recordings which relate to this particular study.

Number/Title	Performer	Location	Tape #
5. I'm Seventeen Come Sunday	Dean Robinson	Brigg, Lincs.	287
12. I'm Seventeen Come Sunday	Dean Robinson	Brigg, Lincs.	287
28. John Bowlin' (Horkstow Grange)	George Gouldthorpe	Brigg, Lincs.	287
2. Lord Melbourne	George Wray		289
4. Lord Melbourne	George Wray		289
12. I'm Seventeen Come Sunday	Edgar Hyldon	Brigg, Lincs.	289
15. Green Bushes	Joseph Leaning	Brigg, Lincs.	289

Number/Title	Performer	Location	Tape #
17. Green Bushes	Joseph Leaning		289
18. Rufford Park Poachers	Joseph Taylor		289
19. I'm Seventeen Come Sunday	Joseph Leaning		289
21. Lisbon (It's on the Monday Morning)	Joseph Leaning		289
22. Dublin Bay (wrong title)	Mr. Dean	Brigg, Lincs.	289
12. John Bowlin' (Harkstow Grange)	George Gouldthorpe		290
8. Seventeen Come Sunday (last verse)	Fred Atkinson	Brigg. Lincs.	291
9. Lost Lady Found	Fred Atkinson	Brigg. Lincs.	291
19. Green Bushes (fragment)	Joseph Leaning		291
2. Green Bushes	Joseph Leaning		292
4. Green Bushes (fragment)	Joseph Leaning		292
21. Brisk Young Sailor (Lady in her Father's Garden)	Mrs. Thompson	Barrow on Humber N.E. Lincs.	292
11. Green Bushes (Twice)	Joseph Leaning		293
14. Lord Melbourne	George Wray		295
4. John Barleycorn	William Short		296
2. Greensleeves	Mr. Bennett (fiddle)	Glos.	299
9. Poaching Song (Lincs. Poacher)	Mrs. Parker	Glos.	299
10. Green Bushes	Mrs. Parker	Glos.	299

Number/Title	Performer	Location	Tape #
15. Higher Germany	Mr. A. Lane	Glos.	299
17. Green Bushes	Mr. Shepherd	Glos.	299
6. Lost Lady Found	Mr. Packlet	Glos.	300
7. A Brisk Young Sailor	Mrs. Packer	Glos.	300
13. Green Bushes	Mr. Shepherd	Glos.	301
1. Claudy Banks	Mr. A. Lane		302

APPENDIX C

FROM SECULAR CHORAL MUSIC IN PRINT

Edited by F. Mark Daugherty and Susan H. Simon
Second Edition, MUSICDATA, Inc., Philadelphia, PA 1987 (in 2 volumes)
(Modern Editions shown in italics)

Blow Away The Morning Dew	SATB	Novello 45.1452.01
Green Bushes	Chorus + Descant	Cramer (G2540)
Greensleeves	SATB	Oxford 53.210 (G2600)
Greensleeves	SA	*Oxford 82.004*
High Germany	Unison Chorus + TTB	Galaxy f.f.(H2535)
I Love My Love	SATB	*G. Schirmer 8117*
I'm Seventeen Come Sunday	SATB	Schott 11339 (G2375)
Lost Lady Found	SATBB, pno/orch	Schott Ed 11284 (G2379)
Pretty Caroline	SS	Novello 48.1770.02 (P2151)
Song of the Blacksmith	Men's Chorus	Curwen 50618 (S5016) *G. Schirmer 11828*
	SATB	Curwen 1086 (S5017) *G. Schirmer 10816*
Swansea Town	Men's Chorus	Curwen 50615 (S7183) *G. Schirmer 8096/8097*
	Mixed Chorus	Curwen 61088 (S7184)

BIBLIOGRAPHY

Baker, Theodore, ed. *Pronouncing Pocket-Manual of Musical Terms* (third revised edition). New York: G. Schirmer, 1947.

Bird, John. *Percy Grainger*. London: Paul Elek, 1976.

Bird, John. *Percy Grainger* (third revised edition). London: Oxford University Press, 1999.

Blom, Eric, ed. *Grove's Dictionary of Music and Musicians*. Vol. 6, *Passacaglia*, by William Barclay Squire. London: MacMillan & Co., Ltd., 1954.

Broadwood, Lucy E. *English Traditional Songs and Carols*. London: Boosey and Co., 1908.

Cantrick, Robert. "Hammersmith and the Two Worlds of Gustav Holst." *Journal of Band Research* 12/2 (1977): 3–11.

Chappell, William. *Popular Music in the Olden Time*. New York: Dover Publications, 1965.

Chater, James. Liner notes from *Danny Boy*. Philips CD 446 657–2, 1996. Compact Disc.

Croft, James. "John Bird's Fascinating Quest to Understand Percy Grainger." *The Instrumentalist* 55/7 (2001): 18–24.

Daugherty, F. Mark, and Simon, Susan H. *Secular Choral Music In Print*, 2 vols. Philadelphia,: Musicdata, Inc., 1987.

Fennell, Frederick. "Gustav Holst's Hammersmith." Basic Band Repertory. *The Instrumentalist* 31/10 (1977): 52–59.

_____. "Gustav Holst's Second Suite in F for Military Band." Basic Band Repertory. *The Instrumentalist* 32/4 (1977): 174–184.

_____. "Molly on the Shore by Percy Aldridge Grainger," Basic Band Repertory. *The Instrumentalist* 38/3 (1983): 24–29.

_____. "Percy Aldridge Grainger's Lincolnshire Posy Part I." Basic Band Repertory. *The Instrumentalist* 34/10 (1980): 42–48.

_____. "Percy Aldridge Grainger's Lincolnshire Posy Part II." Basic Band Repertory. *The Instrumentalist* 35/2 (1980): 15–20.

_____. "Percy Aldridge Grainger's Lincolnshire Posy Part III." Basic Band Repertory. *The Instrumentalist* 35/3 (1980): 28–36.

_____. "Percy Grainger's Irish Tune from County Derry and Shepherd's Hey." Basic Band Repertory. *The Instrumentalist* 33/2 (1978): 18–25.

_____. Personal score to *Hammersmith*. Visit to U.S. Marine Band Library by author, 20 November 1997, Washington, D.C.

_____. "Vaughan Williams' Folk Song Suite." Basic Band Repertory. *The Instrumentalist*, 30/11 (1976): 42–52.

_____. "Vaughan Williams' Toccata Marziale." Basic Band Repertory. *The Instrumentalist*, 31/1 (1976): 44–50.

Garofalo, Robert J. *Guides to Band Masterworks*. Ft. Lauderdale: Meredith Music Publications, 1992.

Grainger, Percy Aldridge. British Folk-Music Settings *Nr. 25 Green Bushes Passacaglia for Two Pianos* (6 Hands). London: Schott and Company, 1921.

_____. "Collecting with the Phonograph." *Journal of the Folk-Song Society*, Vol. 3, 1908–09.

_____. *English Waltz*. San Antonio: Southern Music Company, 1999.

_____. *Lincolnshire Posy*. New York: G. Schirmer, 1940. Reprint Milwaukee: Hal Leonard Publishing Corporation.

_____. *Lincolnshire Posy*. Edited by Frederick Fennell. Cleveland: Ludwig Music Publishing Company, Inc., 1987.

_____. *Molly On The Shore*. New York: Carl Fischer, Inc., 1962. Rev. Critical ed. New York: Carl Fischer, Inc., 2002.

Grauer, Mark. "Grainger's Lost Letters on Lincolnshire Posy." *Instrumentalist* 47/1 (1992): 12–17.

Green, Barry. *The Inner Game of Music*. New York: Bantam Doubleday Dell Publishing Group, Inc., 1986.

Holst, Gustav. *First Suite in E-flat for Military Band, Op. 28 No.1*. London: Boosey and Company, 1921. Rev. ed. London: Boosey and Hawkes Music Publishers Limited, 1984.

_____. "First Suite in E-flat for Military Band, Op. 28 No.1." Facsimile of manuscript score submitted by the composer to Boosey and Company, London. 1909.

_____. *Second Suite in F for Military Band, Op. 28 No.2*. London: Boosey and Company, 1922. Rev. ed. London: Boosey and Hawkes Music Publishers Limited, 1984.

_____. "Second Suite for Military Band in F, Op. 28 No.2." Facsimile of manuscript score submitted by the composer to Boosey and Company, London. 1911.

Holst, Imogen. *The Music of Gustav Holst*. London: Oxford University Press, 1968.

Josephson, David S. Review of *The Wind Music of Percy Aldridge Grainger*, by Thomas Carl Slattery. *Current Musicology* 16 (1973): 79–91.

Karpeles, Maud. *An Introduction to English Folk Song*. London: Oxford University Press, 1973.

Lace, Ian. "Percy Grainger—A Reassessment." *Fanfare* 20/4 (1997): 38, 40, 42, 44, 46, 48.

Leinsdorf, Erich. *The Composer's Advocate, A Radical Orthodoxy for Musicians*. New Haven: Yale University Press, 1981.

Miles, Richard, et al. *Teaching Music Through Performance in Band*. Chicago: GIA Publications, Inc., 1997.

Miles, Richard, et al. *Teaching Music Through Performance in Band, Volume 2*. Chicago: GIA Publications, Inc., 1998.

Miles, Richard, et al. *Teaching Music Through Performance in Band, Volume 3*. Chicago: GIA Publications, Inc., 2000.

Mitchell, Jon C. "Gustav Holst: The Hammersmith Sketches." *College Band Directors National Association Journal* 2/2 (1986): 8–17.

_____. "The Premieres of Hammersmith." *College Band Directors National Association Journal* 1/1 (1984): 18–27.

Norris, Robert S., pastor, Westminster Presbyterian Church. Interview by author, 30 June 1998, Upper St. Clair, PA.

Ould, Barry Peter. Liner notes from *The Grainger Edition, Volume One, Orchestral Works*. Chandos CHAN9493, 1996. Compact Disc.

Reeves, Helen, to Dorothy Sara Lee, 30 November 1981. Grainger Folder, Folklife Reading Room, Library of Congress, Washington, DC.

Sadie, Stanley, ed. *The New Grove Dictionary of Music and Musicians*. Vol 17, *Cecil James Sharp* by Frank Howes. London: MacMillan Publishers Limited, 1980.

_____. *The New Grove Dictionary of Music and Musicians*. Vol 8, *Gustav Holst* by Imogen Holst. London: MacMillan Publishers Limited, 1980.

_____. *The New Grove Dictionary of Music and Musicians*. Vol 3, *Lucy Etheldred Broadwood* by Frank Howes. London: MacMillan Publishers Limited, 1980.

_____. *The New Grove Dictionary of Music and Musicians*. Vol 9, *Maud Karpeles* by Frank Howes. London: MacMillan Publishers Limited, 1980.

_____. *The New Grove Dictionary of Music and Musicians*. Vol 19, *Ralph Vaughan Williams* by Hugh Ottaway. London: MacMillan Publishers Limited, 1980.

Scanzello, Charles J., professor emeritus, Kutztown University. Interview by author, 6 July 1998, Kutztown, PA.

Sharp, Cecil J. *English Folk Songs*, 2 vols. London: Novello and Company, 1921. Reprint 1959.

_____. *English Folk Songs from the Southern Appalachians*. London: Oxford University Press, 1932. Reprint 1952.

_____. 4th Rev. ed. Maud Karpeles. *English Folk Song: Some Conclusions*. Belmont: Wadsworth Publishing Company, Inc., 1965.

_____. *Folk Songs from Somerset*. London: Simpkin and Marshall, 1904.

_____. *One Hundred English Folk Songs*. London: Oliver Ditson Co., 1916. Reprint 1944. Reprint, New York: Dover Pubications, Inc., 1975.

Sharp, Cecil J. and Karpeles, Maud, ed., *Cecil Sharp's Collection of English Folk Songs*. London: Oxford University Press, 1974.

Sharp, Cecil J. and MacIlwaine, Herbert C. *The Morris Book*. Yorkshire: EP Publishing, Limited, 1974.

Smith, Margaret Dean. *A Guide to English Folk Song Collections*. Liverpool: University Press of Liverpool, 1954.

Taylor, Malcom, head librarian Vaughan Williams Memorial Library, London. Phone interview by author, 18 June 1997, Library of Congress, Washington, D.C.

Thompson, Bob. Liner notes from *Unto Brigg Fair*. Joseph Taylor and other traditional Lincolnshire singers recorded by Percy Grainger. Leader LEA 4050, 1908.
Record.

Vaughan Williams, Ralph. *English Folk Song Suite*. London: Boosey and Company,
1924.

_____. *English Folk Song Suite*. Orchestral arrangement Gordon Jacob. London:
Boosey and Company, 1924.

_____. *Five Variants of "Dives and Lazarus"*. London: Oxford University Press,
1940.

_____. Foreword to *English Folk Song: Some Conclusions*, by Cecil J. Sharp. Bel-
mont: Wadsworth Publishing Company, Inc., 1965.

_____. *Sea Songs*. London: Boosey and Company, 1924.

_____. *Toccata Marziale*. London: Boosey and Hawkes, 1924.

Vaughan Williams, Ursula. *R.V.W.—A Biography of Ralph Vaughan Williams*
London: Oxford University Press, 1964.

DISCOGRAPHY

Bishop, Christopher. *Bushes and Briars*. EMI Classics CDMB 65123, 1995. Compact Disc.
  Includes: *Greensleeves, The Song of the Blacksmith, I Love My Love, Swansea Town*.

Boult, Sir Adrian. *Vaughan Williams*. EMI Classics CDM 7 64022 2, 1991. Compact Disc.
  Includes: *English Folk Song Suite* (arr. Gordon Jacob).

Corporon, Eugene. *Tributes*. North Texas Wind Symphony. Klavier Records KCD 11070, 1995. Compact Disc.
  Includes: *Hammersmith*.

_____. *Wildflowers*. North Texas Wind Symphony. Klavier Records KCD 11079, 1996. Compact Disc.
  Includes: *Lincolnshire Posy*.

_____. *Timepieces*. North Texas Wind Symphony. Klavier Records KCD 11122. Compact Disc.
  Includes: *First Suite in E Flat*.

Dunn, Howard. *Dallas Wind Symphony*. Reference Recordings RR-39CD, 1991. Compact Disc.
  Includes: *First Suite in E Flat, Second Suite in F, Hammersmith*.

Fennell, Frederick. *Fanfare and Allegro*. Kosei Publishing Company. KOCD-2811. Compact Disc.
  Includes: *Toccata Marziale*.

_____. *Folksong Suites and other British Band Classics*. Mercury MG50088, 1955. Record.
  Includes: *Second Suite in F, Folk Song Suite*.

_____. *Stars and Stripes*. Telarc CD-80099, 1984. Compact Disc.
  Includes: *Sea Songs, Folk Song Suite, Lincolnshire Posy*.

_____. *The Cleveland Symphonic Winds*. Telarc CD-80038, 1978. Compact Disc.
  Includes: *First Suite in E Flat, Second Suite in F*.

_____. *Winds in Hi-Fi*. Mercury MG50173, 1958. Record
  Includes: *Lincolnshire Posy*.

Gardiner, John Eliot. *Danny Boy.* Philips 446 657-2, 1996. Compact Disc.
    Includes: *I'm Seventeen Come Sunday, The Lost Lady Found.*

Graham, Lieutenant Colonel Lowell E. *Songs of the Earth.* The United States Air
    Force Band BOL 9706, 1997. Compact Disc.
    Includes: *The Duke of Marlborough Fanfare, Lincolnshire Posy.*

Grainger, Percy Aldridge. *Unto Brigg Fair.* Joseph Taylor and other traditional
    Lincolnshire singers recorded by Percy Grainger. Leader LEA 4050, 1908.
    Record.
    Includes: *Rufford Park Poachers, Green Bushes, Horkstow Grange, Lord Melbourne.*
_____. *Percy Grainger Plays Grainger.* Nimbus Records LC5871, 1996. Com-
    pact Disc.
    Includes: *Molly On The Shore.*

Hickox, Richard. *The Grainger Edition, Volume One, Orchestral Works.* Chandos
    CHAN9493, 1996. Compact Disc.
    Includes: *The Duke of Marlborough Fanfare, Green Bushes.*
_____. *The Grainger Edition, Volume Three, Works for Chorus and Orchestra.*
    Chandos CHAN9499, 1996. Compact Disc.
    Includes: *I'm Seventeen Come Sunday.*
_____. *The Grainger Edition, Volume Five, Works for Chorus and Orchestra 2.*
    Chandos CHAN9554, 1997. Compact Disc.
    Includes: *The Lost Lady Found.*
_____. *The Grainger Edition, Volume Six, Orchestral Works 2 The Warriors.* Chan-
    dos CHAN9584, 1997. Compact Disc.
    Includes: *Youthful Suite (English Waltz), Molly On The Shore.*
_____. *Orchestral Works.* London Symphony Orchestra. Chandos CHAN9420,
    1996. Compact Disc.
    Includes: *Hammersmith.*

Hill, Martyn and Thwaites, Penelope. *The Grainger Edition, Volume Seven, Songs for
    Tenor.* Chandos CHAN9610, 1998. Compact Disc.

Hunsberger, Donald. *Eastman Wind Ensemble in Japan, Volume 1.* EMI Toshiba TA
    72043, 1978. Record.
    Includes: *English Folk Song Suite.*
_____. *Live In Osaka—Eastman Wind Ensemble.* Sony Music SK 47198, 1992.
    Compact Disc.
    Includes: *First Suite in E Flat, Lincolnshire Posy.*

Reynish, Timothy and Rundell, Clark. *The Grainger Edition, Volume Four, Works for
    Wind Orchestra.* Chandos CHAN9549, 1997. Compact Disc.
    Includes: *Lincolnshire Posy.*

Reynish, Timothy and Rundell, Clark. *The Grainger Edition, Volume Eight, Works
    for Wind Orchestra 2.* Chandos CHAN9630, 1998. Compact Disc.

Reynolds, H. Robert. *The Retirement Concert April 6, 2001.* University of Michigan
    Symphony Band. Equilibrium, 2001. Compact Disc.
    Includes: *First Suite in E Flat, Lincolnshire Posy.*

Varcoe, Stephen and Thwaites, Penelope. *The Grainger Edition, Volume Two, Songs
    for Baritone.* Chandos CHAN9503, 1996. Compact Disc.
    Includes: *The Lost Lady Found.*

Wick, Denis. *Shepherd's Hey—Wind Music of Grainger—Milhaud–Poulenc.* Academy Sound and Vision Ltd CD WHL 2067, 1992. Compact Disc.
Includes: *Lincolnshie Posy.*

MORE GREAT BOOKS FROM
MEREDITH MUSIC

TEACHING & CONDUCTING RESOURCES

A COMPOSER'S INSIGHT, VOLUME 1
THOUGHTS, ANALYSIS AND COMMENTARY ON CONTEMPORARY MASTERPIECES FOR WIND BAND
edited by Timothy Salzman
A Composer's Insight, Volume 1 – with a foreword by Michael Colgrass – is the first in a five-volume series on major contemporary composers and their works for wind band. Included in this initial volume are rare, "behind-the-notes" perspectives acquired from personal interviews with each composer. An excellent resource for conductors, composers or enthusiasts interested in acquiring a richer musical understanding of the composers' training, compositional approach, musical influences and interpretative ideas. Features the music of: Timothy Broege, Michael Colgrass, Michael Daugherty, David Gillingham, John Harbison, Karel Husa, Alfred Reed and others.
_____00317131 ....$29.95

CONDUCTING WITH FEELING
by Frederick Harris, Jr.
A thought provoking collection of ideas by today's leading conductors on how a conductor develops feelings for a piece of music and communicates those feelings to an ensemble.
_____00317121 ....$18.95

CREATIVE DIRECTOR INTANGIBLES OF MUSICAL PERFORMANCE
by Edward S. Lisk
With a foreword by Mark Camphouse, *Intangibles...* deals with the instructional techniques of teaching expression, ensemble interpretation, characteristic performance, musical identity, and the decision making process surrounding the subtle details of artistic response.
_____00317003 ....$24.95

MUSIC TEACHING STYLE
MOVING BEYOND TRADITION
by Alan Gumm
Music Teaching Style is an exciting, balanced approach to student performance, music learning and personal change. Written in an informal, engaging style, the text is highlighted by anecdotes, quotations, challenges for self-reflection, and techniques used by the author and top professionals in the field. The result – a fulfilling, productive and successful music teaching experience.
_____00317134 ....$34.95

NOTE GROUPING
by James Morgan Thurmond
Fully explains through musical example, the concept of expressive musicianship as taught by Anton Horner, William Kincaid and Marcel Tabuteau. This book clearly illustrates how to teach students to play or sing with expression, musicianship and style and will help to make your performances "come alive".
_____00317028 ....$34.95

ON THE PATH TO EXCELLENCE: THE NORTHSHORE CONCERT BAND
by William S. Carson
From its humble beginnings in 1956, to triumphant concerts in Europe and at the Midwest Clinic, the Northshore Concert Band has led an existence full of twists and turns, adversity and tenacity. How did this group of eleven American Legion musicians evolve into one of the most influential adult bands in history? Follow the story of John Paynter, Barbara Buehlman, and other important musicians as they guide the Northshore Concert Band on the path to excellence.
_____00317135 ....$24.95

TEACHING MUSIC WITH PASSION
CONDUCTING, REHEARSING AND INSPIRING
by Peter Loel Boonshaft
Teaching Music with Passion is a one-of-a-kind, collective masterpiece of thoughts, ideas and suggestions about the noble profession of music education. Both inspirational and instructional, it will surely change the way you teach (and think) about music. Filled with personal experiences, anecdotes and wonderful quotations, this book is an easy-to-read, essential treasure!
_____00317129 ....$24.95

THE WINDS OF CHANGE: THE EVOLUTION OF THE CONTEMPORARY AMERICAN WIND BAND/ENSEMBLE & ITS CONDUCTOR
by Frank Battisti
This expansion on Battisti's *The Twentieth Century American Wind Band/Ensemble* includes discussions on the contribution of important wind band/ensemble personalities and organizations, and provides important information on hundreds of compositions for this medium. Challenges facing the 21st century wind band/ensemble conductor including training and development are also discussed.
_____00317128 ....$34.95

AN UNDERSTANDABLE APPROACH TO MUSICAL EXPRESSION
by Kenneth Laudermilch
Designed to enhance the expressive ability of instrumentalists of every age, this concise, easy-to-understand guide written by Kenneth Laudermilch presents 22 musical concepts that remove the mystery from and provide proficiency in the art of musical expression.
_____00317119 ....$12.95

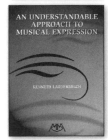

Prices, contents, and availability subject to change without notice.

**For more information on Meredith Music products,
visit www.meredithmusic.com**